I0411786

Quote Octopus
2/53 Barry Street,
Melbourne, Victoria, 3053
Australia
www.quoteoctopus.com

Money has never made man happy, nor will it, there is nothing in its nature to produce happiness. The more of it one has the more one wants.

Benjamin Franklin

A little thought and a little kindness are often worth more than a great deal of money.

John Ruskin

When I was young I thought that money was the most important thing in life; now that I am old I know that it is.

Oscar Wilde

Money won't create success, the freedom to make it will.

Nelson Mandela

Money cannot buy peace of mind. It cannot heal ruptured relationships, or build meaning into a life that has none.

Richard M. DeVos

The lack of money is the root of all evil.

Mark Twain

Wealth is the ability to fully experience life.

Henry David Thoreau

Bottom line is, I didn't return to Apple to make a fortune.
I've been very lucky in my life and already have one.
When I was 25, my net worth was $100 million or so. I
decided then that I wasn't going to let it ruin my life.
There's no way you could ever spend it all, and I don't
view wealth as something that validates my intelligence.

Steve Jobs

Let us not be satisfied with just giving money. Money is
not enough, money can be got, but they need your hearts to
love them. So, spread your love everywhere you go.

Mother Teresa

No one's ever achieved financial fitness with a January
resolution that's abandoned by February.

Suze Orman

A wise man should have money in his head, but not in his

heart.

Jonathan Swift

Greed is not a financial issue. It's a heart issue.

Andy Stanley

Money is only a tool. It will take you wherever you wish, but it will not replace you as the driver.

Ayn Rand

Do what you love and the money will follow.

Marsha Sinetar

There are people who have money and people who are rich.

Coco Chanel

The hardest thing to understand in the world is the income tax.

Albert Einstein

That money talks, I'll not deny, I heard it once: It said, 'Goodbye'.

Richard Armour

The safe way to double your money is to fold it over once and put it in your pocket.

Kin Hubbard

If women didn't exist, all the money in the world would have no meaning.

Aristotle Onassis

The problem is not that people are taxed too little, the problem is that government spends too much.

Ronald Reagan

Real riches are the riches possessed inside.

B. C. Forbes

The American Republic will endure until the day Congress discovers that it can bribe the public with the public's money.

Alexis de Tocqueville

Money makes your life easier. If you're lucky to have it, you're lucky.

Al Pacino

There's no such thing as a free lunch.

Milton Friedman

Here's how I think of my money - as soldiers - I send them out to war everyday. I want them to take prisoners and come home, so there's more of them.

Kevin O'Leary

I have always been afraid of banks.

Andrew Jackson

It's a kind of spiritual snobbery that makes people think they can be happy without money.

Albert Camus

So you think that money is the root of all evil. Have you ever asked what is the root of all money?

Ayn Rand

No complaint... is more common than that of a scarcity of money.

Adam Smith

Ben Franklin may have discovered electricity- but it is the man who invented the meter who made the money.

Earl Warren

Money can't buy love, but it improves your bargaining position.

Christopher Marlowe

Liking money like I like it, is nothing less than mysticism. Money is a glory.

Salvador Dali

A penny saved is a penny earned.

Benjamin Franklin

There is no such thing as a good tax.

Winston Churchill

Sometimes your best investments are the ones you don't make.

Donald Trump

A billion here, a billion there, and pretty soon you're talking about real money.

Everett Dirksen

Money equals freedom.

Kevin O'Leary

A nation that continues year after year to spend more money on military defense than on programs of social uplift is approaching spiritual doom.

Martin Luther King, Jr.

The importance of money flows from it being a link between the present and the future.

John Maynard Keynes

A man in debt is so far a slave.

Ralph Waldo Emerson

A good reputation is more valuable than money.

Publilius Syrus

My pride fell with my fortunes.

William Shakespeare

Money is a strange business. People who haven't got it aim it strongly. People who have are full of troubles.

Ayrton Senna

Honesty is the best policy - when there is money in it.

Mark Twain

Affluence creates poverty.

Marshall McLuhan

It is a waste of money to help those who show no desire to help themselves.

Taylor Caldwell

Money is better than poverty, if only for financial reasons.

Woody Allen

If you want to reap financial blessings, you have to sow financially.

Joel Osteen

He that is of the opinion money will do everything may well be suspected of doing everything for money.

Benjamin Franklin

The thing that differentiates man from animals is money.

Gertrude Stein

If the money we donate helps one child or can ease the pain of one parent, those funds are well spent.

Carl Karcher

Simply by not owning three medium-sized castles in Tuscany I have saved enough money in the last forty years on insurance premiums alone to buy a medium-sized castle in Tuscany.

Ludwig Mies van der Rohe

In suggesting gifts: Money is appropriate, and one size fits all.

William Randolph Hearst

After a certain point, money is meaningless. It ceases to be the goal. The game is what counts.

Aristotle Onassis

All I ask is the chance to prove that money can't make me happy.

Spike Milligan

Many people take no care of their money till they come nearly to the end of it, and others do just the same with their time.

Johann Wolfgang von Goethe

We go to school to learn to work hard for money. I write books and create products that teach people how to have money work hard for them.

Robert Kiyosaki

Poverty makes you sad as well as wise.

Bertolt Brecht

A man with money is no match against a man on a mission.

Doyle Brunson

As human beings, we're very materialistic and have all this stuff - furs and cars and diamonds and money.

Smokey Robinson

A woman's best protection is a little money of her own.

Clare Boothe Luce

Friends and acquaintances are the surest passport to fortune.

Arthur Schopenhauer

It is money, money, money! Not ideas, not principles, but money that reigns supreme in American politics.

Robert Byrd

Everyone needs a certain amount of money. Beyond that, we pursue money because we know how to obtain it. We don't necessarily know how to obtain happiness.

Gregg Easterbrook

It doesn't matter about money; having it, not having it. Or having clothes, or not having them. You're still left alone with yourself in the end.

Billy Idol

Men make counterfeit money; in many more cases, money makes counterfeit men.

Sydney J. Harris

All money means to me is a pride in accomplishment.

Ray Kroc

Money's a horrid thing to follow, but a charming thing to meet.

Henry James

The greatest luxury of riches is that they enable you to escape so much good advice.

Arthur Helps

Recession is when a neighbor loses his job. Depression is when you lose yours.

Ronald Reagan

It is more rewarding to watch money change the world than watch it accumulate.

Gloria Steinem

If saving money is wrong, I don't want to be right!

William Shatner

My goal wasn't to make a ton of money. It was to build good computers.

Steve Wozniak

I'd like to live as a poor man with lots of money.

Pablo Picasso

A bank is a place that will lend you money if you can prove that you don't need it.

Bob Hope

I've got all the money I'll ever need, if I die by four o'clock.

Henny Youngman

Alimony is like buying hay for a dead horse.

Groucho Marx

Money is always there but the pockets change; it is not in the same pockets after a change, and that is all there is to say about money.

Gertrude Stein

Friendship is like money, easier made than kept.

Samuel Butler

I have no money, no resources, no hopes. I am the happiest man alive.

Henry Miller

Profit is sweet, even if it comes from deception.

Sophocles

I am happy to make money. I want to make more money, make more music, eat Big Macs and drink Budweisers.

Kid Rock

Money does not make you happy but it quiets the nerves.

Sean O'Casey

Isn't it a shame that future generations can't be here to see all the wonderful things we're doing with their money?

Earl Wilson

Neither a borrower nor a lender be.

William Shakespeare

Banks have a new image. Now you have 'a friend,' your friendly banker. If the banks are so friendly, how come they chain down the pens?

Alan King

Money often costs too much.

Ralph Waldo Emerson

We've got to put a lot of money into changing behavior.

Bill Gates

Lack of money is the root of all evil.

George Bernard Shaw

Very few people can afford to be poor.

George Bernard Shaw

Money is the barometer of a society's virtue.

Ayn Rand

A man is usually more careful of his money than of his principles.

Oliver Wendell Holmes, Jr.

Anybody who thinks money will make you happy, hasn't got money.

David Geffen

Money is our madness, our vast collective madness.

D. H. Lawrence

It is not the creation of wealth that is wrong, but the love of money for its own sake.

Margaret Thatcher

If God has allowed me to earn so much money, it is because He knows I give it all away.

Edith Piaf

Most men love money and security more, and creation and construction less, as they get older.

John Maynard Keynes

Wealth and want equally harden the human heart.

Theodore Parker

I don't mind that I'm fat. You still get the same money.

Marlon Brando

In its famous paradox, the equation of money and excrement, psychoanalysis becomes the first science to state what common sense and the poets have long known - that the essence of money is in its absolute worthlessness.

Norman O. Brown

Many people are in the dark when it comes to money, and I'm going to turn on the lights.

Suze Orman

Where large sums of money are concerned, it is advisable to trust nobody.

Agatha Christie

I, Joan Crawford, I believe in the dollar. Everything I earn, I spend.

Joan Crawford

There's just one thing I can't figure out. My income tax!

Nat King Cole

Wealth flows from energy and ideas.

William Feather

All riches have their origin in mind. Wealth is in ideas - not money.

Robert Collier

Put not your trust in money, but put your money in trust.

Oliver Wendell Holmes, Sr.

I've made all my money on my own without my family and I work very hard.

Paris Hilton

I am fiercely loyal to those willing to put their money where my mouth is.

Paul Harvey

Many folks think they aren't good at earning money, when what they don't know is how to use it.

Frank A. Clark

The foundation of a financial fresh start actually has nothing to do with money or specific financial dos and don'ts.

Suze Orman

I'm scared to death of being poor. It's like a fat girl who loses 500 pounds but is always fat inside. I grew up poor and will always feel poor inside. It's my pet paranoia.

Cher

A simple fact that is hard to learn is that the time to save money is when you have some.

Joe Moore

What counts is what you do with your money, not where it came from.

Merton Miller

Civilized countries generally adopt gold or silver or both as money.

Alfred Marshall

It is usually people in the money business, finance, and international trade that are really rich.

Robin Leach

Those who are of the opinion that money will do

everything may reasonably be expected to do everything for money.

E. F. L. Wood, 1st Earl of Halifax

I think everything depends on money.

Alan Bean

For I can raise no money by vile means.

William Shakespeare

If you can count your money, you don't have a billion dollars.

J. Paul Getty

No man's credit is as good as his money.

John Dewey

You have to go broke three times to learn how to make a living.

Casey Stengel

A fool and his money are soon parted.

Thomas Tusser

Money differs from an automobile or mistress in being equally important to those who have it and those who do not.

John Kenneth Galbraith

Money is to my social existence what health is to my body.

Mason Cooley

There was a time when a fool and his money were soon parted, but now it happens to everybody.

Adlai E. Stevenson

Money: power at its most liquid.

Mason Cooley

Money just draws flies.

Mahalia Jackson

Nothing is more dangerous to men than a sudden change of fortune.

Quintilian

If I have enough money to eat I'm good.

Shia LaBeouf

Money is a mechanism for control.

David Korten

All my life I knew that there was all the money you could want out there. All you have to do is go after it.

Curtis Carlson

If money was my only motivation, I would organize myself differently.

Placido Domingo

And plenty makes us poor.

John Dryden

I'd rather lose my own money than someone else's.

Dean Kamen

Marrying into money was not a good thing for me.

Anna Nicole Smith

Who covets more is evermore a slave.

Robert Herrick

It was an honor and privilege to arrive to this country 16 years ago with almost no money in my pocket. A lot has happened since then.

Antonio Banderas

It's all about the money.

Joseph Jackson

A fool and his money are lucky enough to get together in the first place.

Stanley Weiser

A man who gives his children habits of industry provides for them better than by giving them fortune.

Richard Whately

Wealth should not be seized, but the god-given is much better.

Hesiod

An important lever for sustained action in tackling poverty and reducing hunger is money.

Gro Harlem Brundtland

If American men are obsessed with money, American women are obsessed with weight. The men talk of gain, the women talk of loss, and I do not know which talk is the more boring.

Marya Mannes

Money is just a way of keeping score.

H. L. Hunt

Sooner or later, we sell out for money.

Tony Randall

It's easier to force feed people than it is to give 'em what they want. It makes more money.

Merle Haggard

Thirteen thousand dollars a year is not enough to raise a family. That's not enough to pay your bills and save for their future. That's barely enough to provide for even the most basic needs.

Thomas Carper

Don't judge me. I made a lot of money.

Samantha Bee

The creditor hath a better memory than the debtor.

James Howell

I don't think business news is just for old white men with money.

Neil Cavuto

Sudden money is going from zero to two hundred dollars a week. The rest doesn't count.

Neil Simon

Business is other people's money.

Delphine de Girardin

I've looked after my money. As I started working around my third birthday, my first check went straight to the bank.

Samantha Barks

You know, a lot of people are just interested in, in building a company so they can make money and get out.

Arthur Rock

Art for art's sake, money for God's sake.

Simon Raven

Many good qualities are not sufficient to balance a single want - the want of money.

Johann Georg Zimmermann

The most efficient labor-saving device is still money.

Franklin P. Jones

You want 21 percent risk free? Pay off your credit cards.

Andrew Tobias

If you make a living, if you earn your own money, you're free - however free one can be on this planet.

Theodore White

Research indicates that most women want their man to earn more than they do.

Laura Schlessinger

I don't spend much money on clothes; I never did.

Lauren Hutton

A fool and his money get a lot of publicity.

Al Bernstein

I think that focusing on the money, on the business, is not enough.

Sergei Bubka

I'm not broke. Like everybody else, I owe money.

Marlee Matlin

A successful man is one who makes more money than his wife can spend. A successful woman is one who can find such a man.

Lana Turner

My favorite things in life don't cost any money. It's really clear that the most precious resource we all have is time.

Steve Jobs

There is only one boss. The customer. And he can fire everybody in the company from the chairman on down, simply by spending his money somewhere else.

Sam Walton

To give real service you must add something which cannot be bought or measured with money, and that is sincerity and integrity.

Douglas Adams

Friends and good manners will carry you where money won't go.

Margaret Walker

Motherhood is a great honor and privilege, yet it is also synonymous with servanthood. Every day women are called upon to selflessly meet the needs of their families. Whether they are awake at night nursing a baby, spending their time and money on less-than-grateful teenagers, or preparing meals, moms continuously put others before themselves.

Charles Stanley

The glow of one warm thought is to me worth more than money.

Thomas Jefferson

In 1985, I was living with my sister in Virginia, and since I was still in high school, I worked at McDonald's to save money to get an abortion. It sounds really terrible, but it was the best decision I ever made. It was the first time I took responsibility for my actions. I messed up, had sex without contraception, and got pregnant at 15.

Kathleen Hanna

The greatest legacy one can pass on to one's children and grandchildren is not money or other material things accumulated in one's life, but rather a legacy of character and faith.

Billy Graham

A business that makes nothing but money is a poor business.

Henry Ford

Allah says in the Qur'an not to despise one another. So the criterion in Islam is not color or social status. It's who is most righteous. If I go to a mosque - and I'm a basketball player with money and prestige - if I go to a mosque and see an imam, I feel inferior. He's better than me. It's about knowledge.

Hakeem Olajuwon

If money is your hope for independence you will never have it. The only real security that a man will have in this world is a reserve of knowledge, experience, and ability.

Henry Ford

Money is not a motivating factor. Money doesn't thrill me or make me play better because there are benefits to being wealthy. I'm just happy with a ball at my feet. My motivation comes from playing the game I love. If I wasn't paid to be a professional footballer I would willingly play for nothing.

Lionel Messi

Money doesn't mean anything to me. I've made a lot of money, but I want to enjoy life and not stress myself building my bank account. I give lots away and live simply, mostly out of a suitcase in hotels. We all know that good health is much more important.

Keanu Reeves

The problem with socialism is that you eventually run out of other peoples' money.

Margaret Thatcher

Making money is art and working is art and good business is the best art.

Andy Warhol

It is not the employer who pays the wages. Employers only handle the money. It is the customer who pays the wages.

Henry Ford

Success comes to those who dedicate everything to their passion in life. To be successful, it is also very important to be humble and never let fame or money travel to your head.

A. R. Rahman

Innovation has nothing to do with how many R & D dollars you have. When Apple came up with the Mac, IBM was spending at least 100 times more on R & D. It's not about money. It's about the people you have, how you're led, and how much you get it.

Steve Jobs

I spent three days a week for 10 years educating myself in

the public library, and it's better than college. People should educate themselves - you can get a complete education for no money. At the end of 10 years, I had read every book in the library and I'd written a thousand stories.

Ray Bradbury

What have I got? No looks, no money, no education. Just talent.

Sammy Davis, Jr.

Let us more and more insist on raising funds of love, of kindness, of understanding, of peace. Money will come if we seek first the Kingdom of God - the rest will be given.

Mother Teresa

Rule No.1: Never lose money. Rule No.2: Never forget rule No.1.

Warren Buffett

Money can buy you a fine dog, but only love can make him wag his tail.

Kinky Friedman

Success isn't measured by money or power or social rank.
Success is measured by your discipline and inner peace.

Mike Ditka

We need business to understand its social responsibility,
that the main task and objective for a business is not to
generate extra income and to become rich and transfer the
money abroad, but to look and evaluate what a
businessman has done for the country, for the people, on
whose account he or she has become so rich.

Vladimir Putin

Money and corruption are ruining the land, crooked
politicians betray the working man, pocketing the profits
and treating us like sheep, and we're tired of hearing
promises that we know they'll never keep.

Ray Davies

It's amazing to me how many people think that voting to
have the government give poor people money is
compassion. Helping poor and suffering people yourself is
compassion. Voting for our government to use guns to
give money to help poor and suffering people is immoral,
self-righteous, bullying laziness.

Penn Jillette

People are sad. People are broke. People are worried about money, people are worried that they're not enough and not amounting to anything and they don't feel good about themselves. People have rough times, and everybody's pretending it's not true, and we need to break that veneer.

Eve Ensler

Money won't buy happiness, but it will pay the salaries of a large research staff to study the problem.

Bill Vaughan

If you work just for money, you'll never make it, but if you love what you're doing and you always put the customer first, success will be yours.

Ray Kroc

I never attempt to make money on the stock market. I buy on the assumption that they could close the market the next day and not reopen it for five years.

Warren Buffett

There's nothing more satisfying than seeing a happy and

smiling child. I always help in any way I can, even if it's just by signing an autograph. A child's smile is worth more than all the money in the world.

Lionel Messi

Money is not the only answer, but it makes a difference.

Barack Obama

My mom worked at McDonald's, and she decided she wanted to make more money, so she got into the management program at McDonald's. And that's how you move up the chain. It's not by demanding that minimum wage is raised; it's by actually acquiring the skills. That's the way that people get ahead in life.

Raul Labrador

Money and success don't change people; they merely amplify what is already there.

Will Smith

Labour was the first price, the original purchase - money that was paid for all things. It was not by gold or by silver, but by labour, that all wealth of the world was originally purchased.

Adam Smith

We have an obligation and a responsibility to be investing in our students and our schools. We must make sure that people who have the grades, the desire and the will, but not the money, can still get the best education possible.

Barack Obama

Tramping is too easy with all this money. My days were more exciting when I was penniless and had to forage around for my next meal... I've decided that I'm going to live this life for some time to come. The freedom and simple beauty of it is just too good to pass up.

Christopher McCandless

Work like you don't need the money. Love like you've never been hurt. Dance like nobody's watching.

Satchel Paige

In fact, the confidence of the people is worth more than money.

Carter G. Woodson

Whoever said money can't buy happiness simply didn't know where to go shopping.

Bo Derek

Advertising is the art of convincing people to spend money they don't have for something they don't need.

Will Rogers

I spent a lot of money on booze, birds and fast cars. The rest I just squandered.

George Best

All money is a matter of belief.

Adam Smith

If nuclear power plants are safe, let the commerical insurance industry insure them. Until these most expert judges of risk are willing to gamble with their money, I'm not willing to gamble with the health and safety of my family.

Donna Reed

Success is having to worry about every damn thing in the world, except money.

Johnny Cash

What's money? A man is a success if he gets up in the morning and goes to bed at night and in between does what he wants to do.

Bob Dylan

I truly believe that women should be financially independent from their men. And let's face it, money gives men the power to run the show. It gives men the power to define value. They define what's sexy. And men define what's feminine. It's ridiculous.

Beyonce Knowles

Attitude is more important than the past, than education, than money, than circumstances, than what people do or say. It is more important than appearance, giftedness, or skill.

Charles R. Swindoll

As for money and prestige, if one has an opportunity to make money and/or advance their position or place in life, there can be a lot to weigh and consider, such as responsibilities, goals and objectives, etc. We all make choices, deal with our sense of priorities, principles, ethics, morals, balancing, juggling, making compromises... or not! Ha!

Axl Rose

For a successful entrepreneur it can mean extreme wealth. But with extreme wealth comes extreme responsibility. And the responsibility for me is to invest in creating new businesses, create jobs, employ people, and to put money aside to tackle issues where we can make a difference.

Richard Branson

I can live without money, but I cannot live without love.

Judy Garland

The American Dream is still alive out there, and hard work will get you there. You don't necessarily need to have an Ivy League education or to have millions of dollars startup money. It can be done with an idea, hard work and determination.

Bill Rancic

I never saw a lawyer yet who would admit he was making money.

Mary Roberts Rinehart

Encouragement to others is something everyone can give. Somebody needs what you have to give. It may not be your money; it may be your time. It may be your listening ear. It may be your arms to encourage. It may be your smile to uplift. Who knows?

Joel Osteen

The way to make money is to buy when blood is running in the streets.

John D. Rockefeller

Companies should not have a singular view of profitability. There needs to be a balance between commerce and social responsibility... The companies that are authentic about it will wind up as the companies that make more money.

Howard Schultz

A real gentleman, even if he loses everything he owns, must show no emotion. Money must be so far beneath a gentleman that it is hardly worth troubling about.

Fyodor Dostoevsky

The circulation of confidence is better than the circulation of money.

James Madison

Most people work just hard enough not to get fired and get paid just enough money not to quit.

George Carlin

Want of money and the distress of a thief can never be alleged as the cause of his thieving, for many honest people endure greater hardships with fortitude. We must therefore seek the cause elsewhere than in want of money, for that is the miser's passion, not the thief s.

William Blake

When we talk about the kind of folks whose lives will be made better by raising the minimum wage, we're not talking about a couple teenagers earning extra spending money to supplement their allowance. We're talking about providers and breadwinners. Working Americans with bills to pay and mouths to feed.

Thomas Perez

Time is money. Wasted time means wasted money means trouble.

Shirley Temple

Teamwork is so important that it is virtually impossible for you to reach the heights of your capabilities or make the money that you want without becoming very good at it.

Brian Tracy

If money help a man to do good to others, it is of some value; but if not, it is simply a mass of evil, and the sooner it is got rid of, the better.

Swami Vivekananda

My dream was to set up my own e-commerce company. In 1999, I gathered 18 people in my apartment and spoke to them for two hours about my vision. Everyone put their money on the table, and that got us $60,000 to start Alibaba. I wanted to have a global company, so I chose a global name.

Jack Ma

Boxing is the only sport you can get your brain shook, your money took and your name in the undertaker book.

Joe Frazier

If you play cricket for India, money is bound to come, and with IPL in and match money of the Ranjhi trophy, I think money is there. There's no good reason why you should not work hard, because at the end of the day, you want to play for your country.

Mahendra Singh Dhoni

I am sure that no man can derive more pleasure from money or power than I do from seeing a pair of basketball goals in some out of the way place.

James Naismith

You can spend the money on new housing for poor people and the homeless, or you can spend it on a football stadium or a golf course.

Jello Biafra

The most valuable lesson I've ever learned in my life is

that life is about family and friends, not about material things or any of that. It's about enjoying your life. If you have no family, no friends to enjoy it with, it don't matter how much you have, how much success you have, how much fame you have, how much money you have, it doesn't matter.

Vanilla Ice

I don't care half so much about making money as I do about making my point, and coming out ahead.

Cornelius Vanderbilt

Rather than love, than money, than fame, give me truth.

Henry David Thoreau

Money can't buy happiness, but it can make you awfully comfortable while you're being miserable.

Clare Boothe Luce

Economics is all about consumption. People either spend money now or they use financial instruments - like bonds, stocks and savings accounts - so they can spend more later.

Adam Davidson

Starbucks is not an advertiser; people think we are a great marketing company, but in fact we spend very little money on marketing and more money on training our people than advertising.

Howard Schultz

Giving money and power to government is like giving whiskey and car keys to teenage boys.

P. J. O'Rourke

Money was never a big motivation for me, except as a way to keep score. The real excitement is playing the game.

Donald Trump

If you don't have integrity, you have nothing. You can't buy it. You can have all the money in the world, but if you are not a moral and ethical person, you really have nothing.

Henry Kravis

Cash - in savings accounts, short-term CDs or money market deposits - is great for an emergency fund. But to fulfill a long-term investment goal like funding your retirement, consider buying stocks. The more distant your financial target, the longer inflation will gnaw at the purchasing power of your money.

Suze Orman

If I win and get the money, then the Oakland Police department is going to buy a boys' home, me a house, my family a house, and a Stop Police Brutality Center.

Tupac Shakur

We don't need new taxes. We need new taxpayers, people that are gainfully employed, making money and paying into the tax system. And then we need a government that has the discipline to take that additional revenue and use it to pay down the debt and never grow it again.

Marco Rubio

I visualise what I want through meditation. The process of meditating is a great way of making sure I have my priorities sorted. It's not about money - I focus on my career and the kind of film projects I want to do. Film-making is a passion for me, and my mantra is that you should do what you love, and the money will follow.

Shilpa Shetty

When I was a deacon, the ominous signs of the Great Depression began to appear. Tens of thousands lost their jobs. Money was scarce. Families had to do without. Some young people did not ask their mothers, 'What's for dinner?' because they knew all too well that their cupboards held very little.

Joseph B. Wirthlin

If you stop at general math, you're only going to make general math money.

Snoop Dogg

That should be the measure of success for everyone. It's not money, it's not fame, it's not celebrity; my index of success is happiness.

Lupe Fiasco

The way money goes so fast these days, they should paint racing stripes on it.

Mark Russell

My parents survived the Great Depression and brought me

up to live within my means, save some for tomorrow, share and don't be greedy, work hard for the necessities in life knowing that money does not make you better or more important than anyone else. So, extravagance has been bred out of my DNA.

David Suzuki

My happiness doesn't come from money or fame. My happiness comes from seeing life without struggle.

Nicki Minaj

You gotta remember: we're musicians... we're just crazy people who can't get along sometimes. I've definitely come to the table with my knife in my pocket a couple of times; you know how it is. It's part of being human. Now add fame and money and all that rock and roll craziness to it - we're lucky we don't eat each other in this industry!

Corey Taylor

I think the person who takes a job in order to live - that is to say, for the money - has turned himself into a slave.

Joseph Campbell

Money can come and go, and fame comes and goes. Peace

of mind and a relationship with God is far more important, so this is the precedent that we've set in our lives. The bottom line is, we all die, so Jesus is the answer.

Phil Robertson

Disneyland is a work of love. We didn't go into Disneyland just with the idea of making money.

Walt Disney

When I was young and it was someone's birthday, I didn't have the money to buy nice presents so I would take my mom's camera and make a movie parody for whoever's birthday it was. When I'd show it them, they'd die laughing. That reaction was a high for me, and I loved that feeling.

David Henrie

Too many people spend money they haven't earned to buy things they don't want to impress people they don't like.

Will Rogers

Half the money I spend on advertising is wasted; the trouble is, I don't know which half.

John Wanamaker

Of the billionaires I have known, money just brings out the basic traits in them. If they were jerks before they had money, they are simply jerks with a billion dollars.

Warren Buffett

The disaster in the Gulf was no accident. It was the result of years of oil money buying off politicians to lead to an unregulated and ill focused addiction to oil and drilling. The doomed fate of the local fisherman and the environment were foretold in the infamous chants of 'Drill, Baby, Drill.'

Robert Greenwald

Don't stay in bed, unless you can make money in bed.

George Burns

People assume I'm out there having this great life, but money doesn't erase the pain. When you're young you barrel through life, making choices without thinking of repercussions. A few years down the line, you wake up in a certain place and wonder how the hell you got there.

Jennifer Lopez

Being good in business is the most fascinating kind of art. Making money is art and working is art and good business is the best art.

Andy Warhol

Despite their good intentions, today's businesses are missing an opportunity to integrate social responsibility and day-to-day business objectives - to do good and make money simultaneously.

Cindy Gallop

People say money ain't nothing; money is basically everything.

Meek Mill

The Internet didn't get invented on its own. Government research created the Internet so that all the companies could make money off the Internet. The point is, is that when we succeed, we succeed because of our individual initiative, but also because we do things together.

Barack Obama

I know of nothing more despicable and pathetic than a man who devotes all the hours of the waking day to the making of money for money's sake.

John D. Rockefeller

There is a gigantic difference between earning a great deal of money and being rich.

Marlene Dietrich

You are your greatest asset. Put your time, effort and money into training, grooming, and encouraging your greatest asset.

Tom Hopkins

If you dream of something worth doing and then simply go to work on it and don't think anything of personalities, or emotional conflicts, or of money, or of family distractions; it is amazing how quickly you get through those 5,000 steps.

Edwin Land

I'm tired of hearing about money, money, money, money, money. I just want to play the game, drink Pepsi, wear Reebok.

Shaquille O'Neal

All the money in the world can't buy you back good health.

Reba McEntire

Maturity: Be able to stick with a job until it is finished. Be able to bear an injustice without having to get even. Be able to carry money without spending it. Do your duty without being supervised.

Ann Landers

Spirituality does two things for you. One, you are forced to become more selfless, two, you trust to providence. The opposite of a spiritual man is a materialist. If I was a materialist I would be making lots of money doing endorsements, doing cricket commentary. I have no interest in that.

Imran Khan

Time is money.

Benjamin Franklin

Love him or hate him, Trump is a man who is certain

about what he wants and sets out to get it, no holds barred. Women find his power almost as much of a turn-on as his money.

Donald Trump

You don't appreciate a lot of stuff in school until you get older. Little things like being spanked every day by a middle-aged woman: Stuff you pay good money for in later life.

Emo Philips

You want to buy cars and houses and castles, all of that's on you and how America has systematized your mind to be into materialism. Hip-hop ain't got nothing to do with that. I'm glad that anybody making money has picked themselves up - I just want them to give some of it back to the community.

Afrika Bambaataa

To get rich, you have to be making money while you're asleep.

David Bailey

Money can't buy life.

Bob Marley

If we pollute the air, water and soil that keep us alive and well, and destroy the biodiversity that allows natural systems to function, no amount of money will save us.

David Suzuki

Most of the people around me have a vested interest in how much money I make. You know, so a celebrity could find themselves in a position where people could have meetings about their life without them involved. And when I say 'their life' I mean not their professional life either. They could talk about their personal life.

Dave Chappelle

I would say the most satisfying thing actually is watching my three children each pick up on their own interests and work many more hours per week than most people that have jobs at trying to intelligently give away that money in fields that they particularly care about.

Warren Buffett

International affairs is very much run like the mafia. The godfather does not accept disobedience, even from a small storekeeper who doesn't pay his protection money. You have to have obedience; otherwise, the idea can spread that you don't have to listen to the orders, and it can spread to important places.

Noam Chomsky

Look at our society. Everyone wants to be thin, but nobody wants to diet. Everyone wants to live long, but few will exercise. Everybody wants money, yet seldom will anyone budget or control their spending.

John C. Maxwell

The Berlin Wall wasn't the only barrier to fall after the collapse of the Soviet Union and the end of the Cold War. Traditional barriers to the flow of money, trade, people and ideas also fell.

Fareed Zakaria

If you don't have your friends and your family, what do you really have? You can have all the money in the world, but with no friends and no family, it's no good.

Meek Mill

I had lost my way for some time, so I need to do things that I am happy with. It's not about being the number one heroine or money. It's about doing roles that I enjoy. My biggest ambition is happiness.

Sonam Kapoor

With our technology, with objects, literally three people in a garage can blow away what 200 people at Microsoft can do. Literally can blow it away. Corporate America has a need that is so huge and can save them so much money, or make them so much money, or cost them so much money if they miss it, that they are going to fuel the object revolution.

Steve Jobs

We have the right as individuals to give away as much of our own money as we please in charity; but as members of Congress we have no right to appropriate a dollar of the public money.

Davy Crockett

The civility which money will purchase, is rarely extended to those who have none.

Charles Dickens

I'm a hard worker, and everything with me is, if I work

hard, I should get paid for it. Everything with me, I try to symbolize something flashy like jewelry or a car. The rubbing hands is a symbol of hustling, so it goes back to the money.

Birdman

I understand what rappers are talking about. I think rap is less about educating people about the black community and more about making money.

Dennis Rodman

I have ways of making money that you know nothing of.

John D. Rockefeller

Knowledge is like money: to be of value it must circulate, and in circulating it can increase in quantity and, hopefully, in value.

Louis L'Amour

Work isn't to make money; you work to justify life.

Marc Chagall

The TV business is uglier than most things. It is normally perceived as some kind of cruel and shallow money trench through the heart of the journalism industry, a long plastic hallway where thieves and pimps run free and good men die like dogs, for no good reason.

Hunter S. Thompson

It's not about how skinny you are or how much money or how many diamonds you have - that's the fluff that people sometimes look at as being the main thing. It's about understanding that the things that make you fabulous are all inside of you.

Kimora Lee Simmons

I'm a good son, a good father, a good husband - I've been married to the same woman for 30 years. I'm a good friend. I finished college, I have my education, I donate money anonymously. So when people criticize the kind of characters that I play on screen, I go, 'You know, that's part of history.'

Samuel L. Jackson

A fascist is one whose lust for money or power is combined with such an intensity of intolerance toward those of other races, parties, classes, religions, cultures, regions or nations as to make him ruthless in his use of deceit or violence to attain his ends.

Henry A. Wallace

I know that campaigns can seem small, and even silly. Trivial things become big distractions. Serious issues become sound bites. And the truth gets buried under an avalanche of money and advertising. If you're sick of hearing me approve this message, believe me - so am I.

Barack Obama

Waste your money and you're only out of money, but waste your time and you've lost a part of your life.

Michael LeBoeuf

Who gets the risks? The risks are given to the consumer, the unsuspecting consumer and the poor work force. And who gets the benefits? The benefits are only for the corporations, for the money makers.

Cesar Chavez

I think that in a year I may retire. I cannot take my money with me when I die and I wish to enjoy it, with my family, while I live. I should prefer living in Germany to any other country, though I am an American, and am loyal to my country.

Harry Houdini

Whoever controls the volume of money in any country is absolute master of all industry and commerce.

James A. Garfield

Money is my military, each dollar a soldier. I never send my money into battle unprepared and undefended. I send it to conquer and take currency prisoner and bring it back to me.

Kevin O'Leary

It takes no compromising to give people their rights. It takes no money to respect the individual. It takes no survey to remove repressions.

Harvey Milk

An athlete cannot run with money in his pockets. He must run with hope in his heart and dreams in his head.

Emil Zatopek

Money can't buy you happiness, but it can buy you a yacht
big enough to pull up right alongside it.

David Lee Roth

Yes I have made a lot of money and I have a lot of respect,
my films have done well, and I know there are loads of
loads of people who look up to me and really love me. I
really just thought this is like a strange dream. I have never
thought this is a success - I don't have a standard.

Shahrukh Khan

If a nation values anything more than freedom, it will lose
its freedom, and the irony of it is that if it is comfort or
money that it values more, it will lose that too.

W. Somerset Maugham

My mom and dad passed away from cancer. Within nine
months, I lost both of my folks. Immediately after that, I
had a horrible betrayal where my brother, who worked for
me, stole a lot of my money. He's in jail now.

Dane Cook

Nothing except the mint can make money without
advertising.

Thomas Babington Macaulay

I believe God wants you to have money to pay your bills, send your kids to college and do charity work and build orphanages. There's the teaching that we're supposed to be poor to show that we're humble. I don't buy that. I think we're supposed to be leaders. We're supposed to excel.

Joel Osteen

There are two things people want more than sex and money... recognition and praise.

Mary Kay Ash

Looking back, yes, I made too many comebacks. But each comeback I was 100 percent sure that I would win. I never came back for the money, because I didn't need it. The adulation I was getting anyway in other spheres. But I'm a guy who likes to see how close he can get to the edge of the mountain - that's what makes me tick.

Sugar Ray Leonard

The companies that survive longest are the one's that work out what they uniquely can give to the world not just growth or money but their excellence, their respect for others, or their ability to make people happy. Some call those things a soul.

Charles Handy

If you love friends, you will serve your friends. If you love community, you will serve your community. If you love money, you will serve your money. And if you love only yourself, you will serve only yourself. And you will have only yourself.

Stephen Colbert

Because women still earn just 77 cents for every dollar men make. Those pennies add up to real money.

Lilly Ledbetter

Money is the worst currency that ever grew among mankind. This sacks cities, this drives men from their homes, this teaches and corrupts the worthiest minds to turn base deeds.

Sophocles

Listen - of course money changes everything, but so does sunlight, and so does food: These are powerful but neutral energy sources, neither inherently good nor evil but shaped only by the way we use them.

Elizabeth Gilbert

Our health care system squanders money because it is designed to react to emergencies. Homeless shelters, hospital emergency rooms, jails, prisons - these are expensive and ineffective ways to intervene and there are people who clearly profit from this cycle of continued suffering.

Pete Earley

The modern banking system manufactures money out of nothing.

Josiah Stamp

The only reason I'm in Hollywood is that I don't have the moral courage to refuse the money.

Marlon Brando

I don't know of any other organization that's raised more money than golf has, because if you are a baseball player, you're a football player, you're a hockey player, if you're just a businessman, and you want to raise some money for a charity, what do they do? They have a golf tournament. They have a golf outing, and they go out and they do it.

Lee Trevino

The writer must earn money in order to be able to live and to write, but he must by no means live and write for the purpose of making money.

Karl Marx

I've lived in many things - boats, caravans, and buses. I've been homeless, I've had no money: everything. But I believe in magic, and having a vision. The tough times made me a warrior. I work hard.

Neon Hitch

I always want to say to people who want to be rich and famous: 'try being rich first'. See if that doesn't cover most of it. There's not much downside to being rich, other than paying taxes and having your relatives ask you for money. But when you become famous, you end up with a 24-hour job.

Bill Murray

Ultimately, if you can say that I'm a bad owner and we're winning championships, I can live with that. But if we're not making the playoffs and we're spending and losing money, then I have to look in the mirror and say maybe I'm not taking the necessary steps to doing what it takes to run an organization.

Michael Jordan

I would prefer to have no money but to have a nice family and good friends around.

Li Na

I do not think I am successful just because I have money. I'm successful because I love who I am and I have no regrets, and I'm successful because I have a great heart and I have compassion and I care and I would be happy with or without money.

Suze Orman

Instead of giving money to found colleges to promote learning, why don't they pass a constitutional amendment prohibiting anybody from learning anything? If it works as good as the Prohibition one did, why, in five years we would have the smartest race of people on earth.

Will Rogers

The extravagant expenditure of public money is an evil not to be measured by the value of that money to the people who are taxed for it.

Chester A. Arthur

God tries you in certain, certain ways. Some people are rich, and they believe in God. They lose the money, things get hard, they get weak and quit going to church. Quit serving God like they did.

Muhammad Ali

Making money is easy. It is. The difficult thing in life is not making it, it's keeping it.

John McAfee

First and foremost I am a drummer. After that, I'm other things... But I didn't play drums to make money.

Ringo Starr

Do not hire a man who does your work for money, but him who does it for love of it.

Henry David Thoreau

When I chased after money, I never had enough. When I

got my life on purpose and focused on giving of myself and everything that arrived into my life, then I was prosperous.

Wayne Dyer

I think it's too bad that everybody's decided to turn on drugs, I don't think drugs are the problem. Crime is the problem. Cops are the problem. Money's the problem. But drugs are just drugs.

Jerry Garcia

When you ain't got no money, you gotta get an attitude.

Richard Pryor

The reason we have poverty is that we have no imagination. There are a great many people accumulating what they think is vast wealth, but it's only money... they don't know how to enjoy it, because they have no imagination.

Alan Watts

There is no class so pitiably wretched as that which possesses money and nothing else.

Andrew Carnegie

If you don't like the idea that most of the money spent on lottery tickets supports government programs, you should know that most of the earnings from mutual funds support investment advisors' and mutual fund managers' retirement.

Robert Kiyosaki

They say Yogi Berra is funny. Well, he has a lovely wife and family, a beautiful home, money in the bank, and he plays golf with millionaires. What's funny about that?

Casey Stengel

Money can add very much to one's ability to lead a constructive life, not only pleasant for oneself, but, hopefully, beneficial to others. My grandfather, along with Carnegie, was a pioneer in philanthropy, which my father then practiced on a very large scale. The Christian ethic played an essential part in my upbringing.

David Rockefeller

In general, the art of government consists of taking as much money as possible from one class of citizens to give to another.

Voltaire

Recommend virtue to your children; it alone, not money, can make them happy. I speak from experience.

Ludwig van Beethoven

As kids we didn't complain about being poor; we talked about how rich we were going to be and made moves to get the lifestyle we aspired to by any means we could. And as soon as we had a little money, we were eager to show it.

Jay-Z

'Untitled' is a time machine that can transport you to 1992, an edgy moment when the art world was crumbling, money was scarce, and artists like Tiravanija were in the nascent stages of combining Happenings, performance art, John Cage, Joseph Beuys, and the do-it-yourself ethos of punk. Meanwhile, a new art world was coming into being.

Jerry Saltz

The first and most imperative necessity in war is money, for money means everything else - men, guns, ammunition.

Ida Tarbell

Never spend your money before you have earned it.

Thomas Jefferson

The Fed should make a clear commitment to stable money to reduce the swings in interest rates and inflation. Instead, it champions and flaunts unstable money. This encourages momentum trading and the growth of derivatives. Meanwhile, layers of financial regulation make Washington bigger and more powerful but don't fix the underlying problems.

David Malpass

The man who won't loan money isn't going to have many friends - or need them.

Wilt Chamberlain

The key to making money is to stay invested.

Suze Orman

The greatest pleasure when I started making money was not buying cars or yachts but finding myself able to have as many freshly typed drafts as possible.

Gore Vidal

I call crony capitalism, where you take money from successful small businesses, spend it in Washington on favored industries, on favored individuals, picking winners and losers in the economy, that's not pro-growth economics. That's not entrepreneurial economics. That's not helping small businesses. That's cronyism, that's corporate welfare.

Paul Ryan

Divorce is one of the most financially traumatic things you can go through. Money spent on getting mad or getting even is money wasted.

Richard Wagner

I think a lot of times it's not money that's the primary motivation factor; it's the passion for your job and the professional and personal satisfaction that you get out of doing what you do that motivates you.

Martin Yan

Whoever decides to dedicate their life to politics knows that earning money isn't the top priority.

Angela Merkel

I wouldn't want to go back over my life. I've done it all. I wouldn't have wanted to miss the Marine Corps. I wouldn't have wanted to miss the war. I wouldn't have missed college. Or playin' for the Colts. I got all the money I need. Five children. I got a truck. I have no regrets whatsoever.

Art Donovan

I went into the business for the money, and the art grew out of it. If people are disillusioned by that remark, I can't help it. It's the truth.

Charlie Chaplin

You shouldn't have to have money to have a luxury fragrance.

Lady Gaga

Everybody gets everything handed to them. The rich inherit it. I don't mean just inheritance of money. I mean what people take for granted among the middle and upper classes, which is nepotism, the old-boy network.

Toni Morrison

Nothing is worse, or more of a breach of the social contract between citizen and state, than for government officials, bureaucrats and agencies to waste the money entrusted to them by the people they serve.

Bob Riley

When we die our money, fame, and honors will be meaningless. We own nothing in this world. Everything we think we own is in reality only being loaned to us until we die. And on our deathbed at the moment of death, no one but God can save our souls.

Michael Huffington

I love to go to Washington - if only to be near my money.

Bob Hope

Liberals, it has been said, are generous with other peoples' money, except when it comes to questions of national survival when they prefer to be generous with other people's freedom and security.

William F. Buckley, Jr.

If you can actually count your money, then you're not a rich man.

J. Paul Getty

My philosophy is that if I have any money I invest it in new ventures and not have it sitting around.

Richard Branson

I just like to keep my money in the bank; I'm not a big risk-taker. I don't know anything about the stock market... I stay away from things I don't know anything about.

Wayne Gretzky

I found this out over the years, that racism is a thinly veiled disguise over economics and money. It really is.

Quincy Jones

Many seniors understand that Social Security is social insurance as opposed to a program where we put money aside for our own retirement. But most elderly individuals think they're getting their money back. So it isn't selfishness as much as a misunderstanding.

Richard Lamm

People don't realize it, but no one lives that rock and roll life 24-7. They think it's hundreds of bottles of champagne flowing and private jets and money. But there's a lot of time when you're traveling - time to think, time to be lonely. Sometimes it gets to you.

Lenny Kravitz

Labor was the first price, the original purchase - money that was paid for all things.

Adam Smith

It's better to waste money, than it is to waste time. You can always get more money.

Hal Sparks

We have this culture of financialization. People think they need to make money with their savings rather with their own business. So you end up with dentists who are more traders than dentists. A dentist should drill teeth and use whatever he does in the stock market for entertainment.

Nassim Nicholas Taleb

Raising the minimum wage to $10.10 will benefit about 28 million workers across the country. And it will help businesses, too - raising the wage will put more money in people's pockets, which they will pump back into the economy by spending it on goods and services in their communities.

Thomas Perez

No one would remember the Good Samaritan if he'd only had good intentions; he had money as well.

Margaret Thatcher

As children, our imaginations are vibrant, and our hearts are open. We believe that the bad guy always loses and that the tooth fairy sneaks into our rooms at night to put money under our pillow. Everything amazes us, and we think anything is possible. We continuously experience life with a sense of newness and unbridled curiosity.

Yehuda Berg

Socialism violates at least three of the Ten Commandments: It turns government into God, it legalizes thievery and it elevates covetousness. Discussions of income inequality, after all, aren't about prosperity but about petty spite. Why should you care how much money I make, so long as you are happy?

Ben Shapiro

I've never been able to understand why a Republican contributor is a 'fat cat' and a Democratic contributor of the same amount of money is a 'public-spirited philanthropist'.

Ronald Reagan

The first time you marry for love, the second for money, and the third for companionship.

Jackie Kennedy

There's something about a holiday that isn't all about how much money you spend.

Hilarie Burton

Making money is a hobby that will complement any other hobbies you have, beautifully.

Scott Alexander

I think it's way harder when you have success, 'cause people tend to not treat you the same or look at you the same because they see the success or the money you make.

Meek Mill

Money doesn't make you happy. I now have $50 million but I was just as happy when I had $48 million.

Arnold Schwarzenegger

I always thought money was something just to make me happy. But I've learned that I feel better being able to help my folks, 'cause we never had nothing. So just to see them excited about my career is more of a blessing than me actually having it for myself.

Kendrick Lamar

If we were motivated by money, we would have sold the company a long time ago and ended up on a beach.

Larry Page

You reach a point where you don't work for money.

Walt Disney

You can't reverse fame. You can lose all the money, but you'll never lose people knowing you.

J. Cole

Property may be destroyed and money may lose its
purchasing power; but, character, health, knowledge and
good judgement will always be in demand under all
conditions.

Roger Babson

I'd asked around 10 or 15 people for suggestions. Finally
one lady friend asked the right question, 'Well, what do
you love most?' That's how I started painting money.

Andy Warhol

The times of Arab nationalism and unity are gone forever.
These ideas which mobilized the masses are only a
worthless currency. Libya has had to put up with too much
from the Arabs for whom it has poured forth both blood
and money.

Muammar al-Gaddafi

I don't care about having money. It's about being happy,
man.

Skrillex

For the past few years, I've been more selective than I have any right to be, but I think that's finally starting to work in my favor. I think I get way too much credit for making what people consider to be smart choices, but it's only because I made a decision to stop worrying about making money.

Lizzy Caplan

One might think that the money value of an invention constitutes its reward to the man who loves his work. But... I continue to find my greatest pleasure, and so my reward, in the work that precedes what the world calls success.

Thomas A. Edison

In liberal logic, if life is unfair then the answer is to turn more tax money over to politicians, to spend in ways that will increase their chances of getting reelected.

Thomas Sowell

Many novice real estate investors soon quit the profession and invest in a well-diversified portfolio of bonds. That's because, when you invest in real estate, you often see a side of humanity that stocks, bonds, mutual funds, and saving money shelter you from.

Robert Kiyosaki

Making money is a happiness. And that's a great incentive. Making other people happy is a super-happiness.

Muhammad Yunus

Productivity - the amount of output delivered per hour of work in the economy - is often viewed as the engine of progress in modern capitalist economies. Output is everything. Time is money. The quest for increased productivity occupies reams of academic literature and haunts the waking hours of C.E.O.s and finance ministers.

Tim Jackson

Time is money says the proverb, but turn it around and you get a precious truth. Money is time.

George Gissing

I try to give to the poor people for love what the rich could get for money. No, I wouldn't touch a leper for a thousand pounds; yet I willingly cure him for the love of God.

Mother Teresa

This is our commitment to users and the people who use our service, is that Facebook's a free service. It's free now. It will always be free. We make money through having advertisements and things like that.

Mark Zuckerberg

You may earn whatever money you earn as a cricketer, but you want to play for your country. At the end of the day, you want to do something special. There are plenty of people who earn 50 crores or 100 crores as businessmen or big professionals or who are really doing well in business. But what gives pleasure to your mom and dad is the fame.

Mahendra Singh Dhoni

Fashion is an industry to make money. It plays into human psychology. We want to belong, we want to be loved. I'm not trying to demonize the fashion industry - I love the fashion industry - but style is about taking the control out of the industry's hand and having you decide what works for you.

Stacy London

If you didn't have patents, no one would bother to spend money on research and development. But with patents, if someone has a good idea and a competitor can't copy it, then that competitor will have to think of their own way of doing it. So then, instead of just one innovator, you have two or three people trying to do something in a new way.

James Dyson

You loan your friend money. You see them again, they don't say nothin' 'bout the money. 'Hi, how ya doin'? How's ya mama doing?' Man, how's my money doin'?

Chris Tucker

It's hard to tell with these Internet startups if they're really interested in building companies or if they're just interested in the money. I can tell you, though: If they don't really want to build a company, they won't luck into it. That's because it's so hard that if you don't have a passion, you'll give up.

Steve Jobs

I made more money yesterday than I ever thought I'd make in an entire lifetime. But it's like somebody's going to take it all away from me and I'll be back in Texas, installing them damned irrigation wells. I didn't like that when I was sixteen. And I know I wouldn't like it when I'm eighty.

Jimmy Dean

Money you won't need to use for at least seven years is money for investing. The goal here is to have your account grow over time to help you finance a distant goal, such as building a retirement fund. Since your goal is in the future, money for investing belongs in stocks.

Suze Orman

I just feel like, with rappers, there's so much complacency. It's like, 'Oh, I'm a rapper. I'm successful. I make money. That's all that matters.' But there's a lot of stuff going on in the world. Whether or not you're aware of it, it's happening.

J. Cole

No hours, nor amount of labor, nor amount of money would deter me from giving the best that there was in me.

Colonel Sanders

If all the rich and all of the church people should send their children to the public schools they would feel bound to concentrate their money on improving these schools until they met the highest ideals.

Susan B. Anthony

The big difference between sex for money and sex for free is that sex for money usually costs a lot less.

Brendan Behan

Athletes and musicians make astronomical amounts of money. People get paid $100 million to throw a baseball! Shouldn't we all take less and pass some of that money onto others? Think about firefighters, teachers and policemen. We should celebrate people that are intellectually smart and trying to make this world a better place.

Kid Rock

In my view, a philanthropist is anyone who gives anything - time, money, experience, skills or networks - in any amount, to create a better world. This is not how we once thought about philanthropy. The word used to conjure up something rather passive - sitting down and writing checks.

Laura Arrillaga-Andreessen

I'm no good at anything but comedy, which I think I'm good at. I'm absolutely no good at networking; I'm terrible at acting; I'm terrible at dealing with executives; I'm terrible at collaborating. And I say whatever I want to say. But I think I'm good enough at comedy that I can survive.

And I don't really have an ambition for money.

Norm MacDonald

People see me as a person who can make them some money, which makes it hard to make real friends. I'm asked to do a lot of stuff for free - to wear certain clothes, turn up to events - people use you to make money. I think that's why I tend to jump into relationships.

Sophie Monk

Money is human happiness in the abstract; he, then, who is no longer capable of enjoying human happiness in the concrete devotes himself utterly to money.

Arthur Schopenhauer

If you don't want to work you have to work to earn enough money so that you won't have to work.

Ogden Nash

No woman marries for money; they are all clever enough, before marrying a millionaire, to fall in love with him first.

Cesare Pavese

You should breathe deeply and chant, 'Money will easily and effortlessly flow into my life' as often as you can every day. Things will start to change after a month. If you believe you will be financially secure, then you are opening yourself up to change.

Louise L. Hay

Poverty is multidimensional. It extends beyond money incomes to education, health care, political participation and advancement of one's own culture and social organisation.

Atal Bihari Vajpayee

Whenever people with money have power over people with less money, you have the potential for exploitation.

Jennifer Weiner

I was a common man, and I will always remain a common man. No amount of stardom will ever consume my soul. Money comes, money goes. Fame comes, fame goes. I believe every human being is a celebrity in their own right.

A. R. Rahman

Writing is like prostitution. First you do it for love, and

then for a few close friends, and then for money.

Moliere

The darkest hour in any man's life is when he sits down to plan how to get money without earning it.

Horace Greeley

If you put all your strength and faith and vigor into a job and try to do the best you can, the money will come.

Lawrence Welk

While money doesn't buy love, it puts you in a great bargaining position.

Christopher Marlowe

As they say around the Texas Legislature, if you can't drink their whiskey, screw their women, take their money, and vote against 'em anyway, you don't belong in office.

Molly Ivins

I don't really care about money. I find money boring and accounting boring, so I'm probably not going to ever make a lot of money.

Juliana Hatfield

I have learned so many things from my mother about the right upbringing, the right values, value for money, value for elders, for family members. I think these things only a parent can teach you.

Karisma Kapoor

Money doesn't make people happy. People make people happy.

Steve Wynn

Unless you're living on the street and surviving on a diet of discarded turkey drumsticks, there's no point in being gloomy. We've spent too long trying to cheer ourselves up by spending money on brightly coloured things we don't really need. We've stopped using our imaginations.

Jarvis Cocker

Even though the money is great and the fame is great, you still have a lot of disenfranchised young men that are participating in the NFL that are not very happy. A lot of them are very bitter. A lot them are very angry. So many of them have had no fathers and no home life, and basically, no education.

Jim Brown

I don't want to be married to someone who feels inferior to my success or because I make more money than he does.

Grace Kelly

Hating Wall Street is an American tradition that dates back even to the days when Thomas Jefferson cursed that money lover Alexander Hamilton. And for centuries, the complaints about it have largely stayed the same: 'It does nothing! It creates chaos! It's a parasite that sucks hardworking Americans dry!'

Adam Davidson

My mother was an English teacher who decided to become a math teacher, and she used me as a guinea pig at home. My father had been a math teacher and then went to work at a steel mill because, frankly, he could make more money doing that.

Freeman A. Hrabowski III

I don't want to be in somebody else's movie, and then they

make all the money. I've gotten offers to do the movies, but I won't sell myself short and be in somebody else's movie, like 'Boyz N the Hood.' I don't think I woulda done that.

Eazy-E

God wants us to prosper financially, to have plenty of money, to fulfill the destiny He has laid out for us.

Joel Osteen

When it is a question of money, everybody is of the same religion.

Voltaire

Business, that's easily defined - it's other people's money.

Peter Drucker

People spend time worrying about things they think they have to have and lose perception of what they do have. You can have all the money and material things you want. If you aren't here to enjoy them, what good do they do?

Eric Davis

I advise everybody not to save: spend your money. Most people save all their lives and leave it to somebody else. Money is to be enjoyed.

Hedy Lamarr

The parents have a right to say that no teacher paid by their money shall rob their children of faith in God and send them back to their homes skeptical, or infidels, or agnostics, or atheists.

William Jennings Bryan

A moderate addiction to money may not always be hurtful; but when taken in excess it is nearly always bad for the health.

Clarence Day

Our public school system is our country's biggest and most inefficient monopoly, yet it keeps demanding more and more money.

Phyllis Schlafly

There's so much importance in honoring your everyday hero. It doesn't take money. It doesn't take connections. What matters is that people get involved. Whether your passion is gun control or food or whatever it may be, everybody needs to stop being so self-absorbed.

Debi Mazar

There is hardly any money interest in art, and music will be there when money is gone.

Duke Ellington

Time is money, especially when you are talking to a lawyer or buying a commercial.

Frank Dane

I'm a little lavish I must admit. But I'm not really concerned with money. Being rich is not my goal, being wealthy is.

Cee Lo Green

Good grooming is integral and impeccable style is a must. If you don't look the part, no one will want to give you time or money.

Daymond John

Democrats are people who raise your taxes and spend your money on weird stuff. They steal your guns, and they spit on your faith. And because the Democratic Party was taken over by the aggressive secular guys, they became hostile not just to conservative Catholics and evangelical Christians, but Orthodox Jews and Muslims and Mormons.

Grover Norquist

You don't want to have so much money going toward your mortgage every month that you can't enjoy life or take care of your other financial responsibilities.

Dave Ramsey

Could a government dare to set out with happiness as its goal? Now that there are accepted scientific proofs, it would be easy to audit the progress of national happiness annually, just as we monitor money and GDP.

Polly Toynbee

The highest use of capital is not to make more money, but to make money do more for the betterment of life.

Henry Ford

I don't make deals for the money. I've got enough, much

more than I'll ever need. I do it to do it.

Donald Trump

A system of capitalism presumes sound money, not fiat money manipulated by a central bank. Capitalism cherishes voluntary contracts and interest rates that are determined by savings, not credit creation by a central bank.

Ron Paul

Portland is quickly becoming one of those lovely, lush Third World countries where kinda-rich people retire with their money.

Chuck Palahniuk

It's like, hmm, there's people with $2000 weaves that could have bought health care with that weave money. They don't have insurance. People want what they want. And I guess that is a reason we have this big credit card problem and a lot of these foreclosures.

Chris Rock

False opinions are like false money, struck first of all by guilty men and thereafter circulated by honest people who perpetuate the crime without knowing what they are doing.

Joseph de Maistre

Unfortunately, corruption is widespread in government agencies and public enterprises. Our political system promotes nepotism and wasting money. This has undermined our legal system and confidence in the functioning of the state. One of the consequences is that many citizens don't pay their taxes.

George Papandreou

The notion of making money by popular work, and then retiring to do good work, is the most familiar of all the devil's traps for artists.

Logan Pearsall Smith

I believe that anybody who gets married should go to a counselor for months before the wedding. I think that's going to save guys a lot of money and the ladies a lot of heartbreak.

James Brolin

Zoroastrianism is about the opposition of good and evil. For the triumph of good, we have to make a choice. We can enlist on the side of good by prospering, making money and using our wealth to help others.

Rohinton Mistry

One can understand a person by the way he removes his wallet and puts his hand to take out money.

Boman Irani

When you talk about the oil wealth you compare nations. There are some nations with less than five million people. Nigeria has 150 million people. I cannot say that all the money earned from oil since 1958, when the first drop of oil was exported from this country to date, that the money has been effectively used.

Goodluck Jonathan

I wish people would spend their money on hybrid cars.

Ryan Tedder

This will never be a civilized country until we spend more money for books than we do for chewing gum.

Elbert Hubbard

My challenge when I came back was to face the young talent, dissect their games, and show them maybe that they needed to learn more about the game than just the money aspect.

Michael Jordan

Time and money spent in helping men to do more for themselves is far better than mere giving.

Henry Ford

Why is there so much month left at the end of the money?

John Barrymore

There is no virtue in compulsory government charity, and there is no virtue in advocating it. A politician who portrays himself as 'caring' and 'sensitive' because he wants to expand the government's charitable programs is merely saying that he's willing to try to do good with other people's money.

P. J. O'Rourke

I'm not a driven businessman, but a driven artist. I never think about money. Beautiful things make money.

Lord Acton

American men, as a group, seem to be interested in only two things, money and breasts. It seems a very narrow outlook.

Hedy Lamarr

My mother was a public school teacher in Virginia, and we didn't have any money, we just survived on happiness, on being a happy family.

Dave Grohl

We're throwing money down a rat hole drain of public education! We lead the world in public education spending. We lead the world in getting the least for it.

Rush Limbaugh

Print some money and give it to us for the rain forests.

Vivienne Westwood

No money on earth can buy the love and affection that has been given to me by a grateful nation.

Abdul Qadeer Khan

Most of Hollywood is about making money - and I love money, but I don't make the films thinking about money.

David Lynch

I choose the likely man in preference to the rich man; I want a man without money rather than money without a man.

Themistocles

When I was 16 I'd watch 'The Godfather,' but I didn't think, 'Right, I'm going to go down the barber's and get some protection money off him.'

Noel Gallagher

As women, we all have certain weaknesses. I know one who can't resist pretty shoes but has nothing suitable to wear with them. Others adore frilly lingerie but never have any money to buy outer clothing.

Edith Head

Try paying the bills with love. The idea I am trying to

espouse is that you can have both love and money, and be rich and generous.

T. Harv Eker

Don't cling to fame. You're just borrowing it. It's like money. You're going to die, and somebody else is going to get it.

Sonny Bono

Companies spend millions of dollars on firewalls, encryption, and secure access devices and it's money wasted because none of these measures address the weakest link in the security chain: the people who use, administer, operate and account for computer systems that contain protected information.

Kevin Mitnick

I want 'Vogue' to be pacy, sharp, and sexy - I'm not interested in the super-rich or infinitely leisured. I want our readers to be energetic executive women, with money of their own and a wide range of interests. There is a new kind of woman out there. She's interested in business and money.

Anna Wintour

In 1975, when my students were kidnapped by rebels, I was accused of hiding instead of trying to save them, and of not giving enough money for their ransom. I wasn't believed.

Jane Goodall

I've had a tough time learning how to act like a congressman. Today I accidentally spent some of my own money.

Joseph P. Kennedy

My best investment, as cliched as this sounds, is the money I've spent developing myself, via books, workshops and coaching. Leadership begins within, and to have a better career, start by building a better you.

Robin S. Sharma

You have to manage money. Particularly with market economies. You may have a great product, but if your bottom line goes bust, then that's it.

Mukesh Ambani

At first, we couldn't be establishment, because we didn't have any money. We were guerrilla marketers, and we still are, a little bit. But, as we became No. 1 in our industry, we've had to modify our culture and become a bit more planned.

Phil Knight

But nothing is better than the market, where the customer and the business deal directly with each other, because if you rip people off, word gets out. That business eventually loses its customers, and the good ones that serve people well get the business. You get government in there, and it's just more money for the lawyers who write the bills.

John Stossel

But with lots of good ideas, implementation is the key, and so we need to keep our eye on the ball as we go forward and make sure that people honor their pledges in terms of financial commitments, and that we actually use this money so that it makes a real difference.

Mitchell Reiss

Money is not required to buy one necessity of the soul.

Henry David Thoreau

When a man says money can do anything, that settles it: he

hasn't got any.

George Bernard Shaw

Measure your wealth by what you'd have left if you lost all your money.

H. Jackson Brown, Jr.

Business, you know, may bring you money, but friendship hardly ever does.

Jane Austen

You have reached the pinnacle of success as soon as you become uninterested in money, compliments, or publicity.

Thomas Wolfe

Nowadays nothing but money counts: a fortune brings honors, friendships; the poor man everywhere lies low.

Ovid

I will not play just an evil part. In fact, I got offered $7 million several years ago to play the part that Faye Dunaway played in 'Supergirl.' I was kind of insulted. I was impressed with the money, but I said, 'Why are you asking me to play an evil witch? Do I come across as an evil witch to you?'

Dolly Parton

Anyone who wants to sell you overnight success or wealth is not interested in your success; they are interested in your money.

Bo Bennett

If one man in the country could take all the money, what was the use of passing any bills about it?

Davy Crockett

Before borrowing money from a friend it's best to decide which you need most.

Joe Moore

The only rich person is a person who is rich in spirit. I have no money deposit. I have only beauty deposit.

Imelda Marcos

I definitely don't think that money can buy you love. It can buy you affection but certainly not love.

George Best

Long Kiss Goodnight has a huge cult following. They could make another version of that movie right now and make a lot of money.

Samuel L. Jackson

Research is four things: brains with which to think, eyes with which to see, machines with which to measure and, fourth, money.

Albert Szent-Gyorgyi

But it's a blessing to be so successful within a year; it's the greatest feeling in the world, making money and doing the things that I'm doing, and I definitely trying to continue doing what I'm doing.

Ludacris

Team Obama continues to dominate new media, spending far more effort and money than Team Romney in targeted online youth outreach.

Jennifer Granholm

The best money advice ever given me was from my father. When I was a little girl, he told me, 'Don't spend anything unless you have to.'

Dinah Shore

Do the elected officials in Washington stand with ordinary Americans - working families, children, the elderly, the poor - or will the extraordinary power of billionaire campaign contributors and Big Money prevail? The American people, by the millions, must send Congress the answer to that question.

Bernie Sanders

I never look at it like I'm wasting money when I'm buying gold.

Big Sean

An influential member of parliament has not only to pay much money to become such, and to give time and labour, he has also to sacrifice his mind too - at least all the characteristics part of it that which is original and most his own.

Walter Bagehot

Advertising is totally unnecessary. Unless you hope to make money.

Jef I. Richards

It's an irony that growing inequality could mean more money for philanthropy. In the U.S., quite a few of the ultra-rich have taken to heart the 19th century industrialist and philanthropist Andrew Carnegie's comment that it's a disgrace to die wealthy.

Geoff Mulgan

The goal isn't how much money you make, but how much you help people.

Blake Mycoskie

Get that right, then- if you get the quality right, then the marketability or whatever; your ability to sell videos or your ability to earn money or whatever, will follow naturally. But try to be creatively lead rather than market lead. And that's important to me.

Rowan Atkinson

We have over 500,000 illegal immigrants living in Arizona. And we simply cannot sustain it. It costs us a tremendous amount of money of course in health care, in education, and then, on top of it all, in incarceration. And the federal government doesn't reimburse us on any of these things.

Jan Brewer

Americans spend more money on Botox, face lifts and tummy tucks than on the age-old scourges of polio, small pox and malaria.

Victor Davis Hanson

Don't give me any money, don't give me any people, but give freedom, and I'll give you a movie that looks gigantic.

Robert Rodriguez

The more money the louder it talks.

Arnold Rothstein

There seems to be an inclination among rock musicians to be very carefree with money, but I negotiate the best flight and hotel deals on our tours to maximise the band's income - I don't want too see too much taken off the top line.

Ian Anderson

There's competition in every field, and that's healthy. It makes you work harder and be your best. Competition, not in terms of money or number of projects, but in the quality of your work, is very healthy.

Katrina Kaif

I think we're returning to more of the original vibration of music and creativity through the removal of this distortion called the music industry. That's where we're heading. And it'll cut out a lot of music if people ever expected to make money.

Jane Siberry

We Hoosiers hold to some quaint notions. Some might say we 'cling' to them, though not out of fear or ignorance. We believe in paying our bills. We have kept our state in the black throughout the recent unpleasantness, while cutting rather than raising taxes, by practicing an old tribal ritual - we spend less money than we take in.

Mitch Daniels

After 'Chandni Bar' there was a shutdown of such bars in Mumbai. After 'Page 3' people started avoiding such events. 'Traffic Signal' exposed the money flow through the mafia. I'm not apologetic about the brutal truth in my films. Almost 70% of my films are based on reality, and 30% I fictionalize or change to suit my film.

Madhur Bhandarkar

When you are writing a song for something else, if you are doing something for money, I always think that's bad luck.

Chad Kroeger

I think I matured quite early, but what that does mean is I have moments of complete immaturity. When I come home, I don't want to be an actor. I just want to be a kid. I barely even know what money is.

Dakota Blue Richards

What kind of moron would go to work for half the amount of money, when they could sit at home and collect what's written in a contract?

Bill Goldberg

One of the things about animal rights, which is not the

only thing that I care about in this world, is that your money can bring success. I see results.

Sam Simon

Government can wreck a business by confiscating its money by taxation.

Owen Paterson

I say 20 words in English. I say money, money, money, and I say hot dog! I say yes, no and I say money, money, money and I say turkey sandwich and I say grape juice.

Carmen Miranda

It is a kind of spiritual snobbery that makes people think they can be happy without money.

Albert Camus

I'm just trying to be the me that I am and not all of this other crap. I just want to be the family man, and if somehow I can make the money to get my ranch and get the hell away from everybody else, that would be awesome.

Chris Kyle

Money has to serve, not to rule.

Pope Francis

Making money is certainly the one addiction I cannot shake.

Felix Dennis

There was one thing my daddy wouldn't tolerate in any shape, form or fashion, and that was being unkind or rude to somebody. That was just very important to my folks. And as it turns out, that was a legacy that he left me that money can't buy, is how to be able to treat people.

Paula Deen

Words are the money of fools.

Thomas Hobbes

Money, not morality, is the principle commerce of civilized nations.

Thomas Jefferson

There are three faithful friends - an old wife, an old dog, and ready money.

Benjamin Franklin

In any investment, you expect to have fun and make money.

Michael Jordan

One does not need buildings, money, power, or status to practice the Art of Peace. Heaven is right where you are standing, and that is the place to train.

Morihei Ueshiba

Some of you may know my story: How for nineteen years, I worked as a manager for a tire plant in Alabama. And some of you may have lived a similar story: After nearly two decades of hard, proud work, I found out that I was making significantly less money than the men who were doing the same work as me.

Lilly Ledbetter

We can be thankful to a friend for a few acres, or a little money; and yet for the freedom and command of the whole earth, and for the great benefits of our being, our life, health, and reason, we look upon ourselves as under no obligation.

Lucius Annaeus Seneca

You've got to tell your money what to do or it will leave.

Dave Ramsey

I have wasted the greater part of my life looking for money and trying to get along, trying to make my work from this terribly expensive paintbox, which is a movie. And I've spent too much energy on things that have nothing to do with making a movie. It's about two percent moviemaking and ninety-eight percent hustling It's no way to spend a life.

Orson Welles

I'm fulfilled in what I do. I never thought that a lot of money or fine clothes - the finer things of life - would make you happy. My concept of happiness is to be filled in a spiritual sense.

Coretta Scott King

We have the best government that money can buy.

Mark Twain

A rich man is nothing but a poor man with money.

W. C. Fields

Nobody climbs mountains for scientific reasons. Science is used to raise money for the expeditions, but you really climb for the hell of it.

Edmund Hillary

The riches of the game are in the thrills, not the money.

Ernie Banks

A guy's who has all the money he needs and never faced any hard times, he won't have any character. But when you've had it tough and you've had it rough and you thought you were at the end of the rope and you work your way out of it, that's the way you build character.

Bobby Bowden

At the heart of banking is a suicidal strategy. Banks take money from the public or each other on call, skim it for their own reward and then lock the rest up in volatile, insecure and illiquid loans that at times they cannot redeem without public aid.

James Buchan

A film like 'Good Night And Good Luck,' you make that for $7 million because you know it's a black-and-white film, and it's not an easy sell. If you make it for $7 million, then everybody can have a chance to make a little bit of money, and you get to make the film you want to make.

Grant Heslov

A fool and his money are soon elected.

Will Rogers

I've always felt toward the slightest scene, even if all I had to do in a scene was just to come in and say, 'Hi,' that the people ought to get their money's worth and that this is an obligation of mine, to give them the best you can get from me.

Marilyn Monroe

Time well spent results in more money to spend, more money to save, and more time to vacation.

Zig Ziglar

As one digs deeper into the national character of the Americans, one sees that they have sought the value of everything in this world only in the answer to this single question: how much money will it bring in?

Alexis de Tocqueville

Capital is money, capital is commodities. By virtue of it being value, it has acquired the occult ability to add value to itself. It brings forth living offspring, or, at the least, lays golden eggs.

Karl Marx

The worship of the golden calf of old has found a new and heartless image in the cult of money and the dictatorship of an economy which is faceless and lacking any truly human goal.

Pope Francis

We do not have a money problem in America. We have a values and priorities problem.

Marian Wright Edelman

Money doesn't buy elegance. You can take an inexpensive sheath, add a pretty scarf, gray shoes, and a wonderful bag, and it will always be elegant.

Carolina Herrera

When I decided to be a musician I reckoned that that was going to be the way of less profit, less money. I was sort of giving up the idea of making a lot of money. It was what I loved to do. I would have done it anyway. If I'd had to work at Taco Bell I'd have still been out at night trying to play music.

Tom Petty

If a man has wealth, he has to make a choice, because there is the money heaping up. He can keep it together in a bunch, and then leave it for others to administer after he is dead. Or he can get it into action and have fun, while he is still alive. I prefer getting it into action and adapting it to human needs, and making the plan work.

George Eastman

I sat with him for three hours and we did not exchange a single word. At the end he handed me, as he had done before, an envelope with money in it. It would have been much nicer if he had enclosed a greeting or a loving word. I would have been so pleased if he had.

Eva Braun

The president has been a true friend of the ag industry, because he continues to invest large amounts of money at a time when savings is really the goal of the federal government to deal with the deficit.

Mike Johanns

There's no way in the world I can feel the same blues the way I used to. When I play in Chicago, I'm playing up-to-date, not the blues I was born with. People should hear the pure blues - the blues we used to have when we had no money.

Muddy Waters

There is only one class in the community that thinks more about money than the rich, and that is the poor. The poor can think of nothing else.

Oscar Wilde

Money is neither my god nor my devil. It is a form of energy that tends to make us more of who we already are, whether it's greedy or loving.

Dan Millman

Demographics show that we are entering a battle between young and old. I call it the 'Age War.' The young want to hang onto their money to grow their families, businesses, and wealth. The old want the tax and investment dollars of the young to sustain their old age.

Robert Kiyosaki

I'm free of stress and worries now because if I don't like something I'm doing, I just find the fun in it instead of being miserable. Let me have fun with the people I work with, let me have fun making money - when I grew up so poor, ya know?

Jenny McCarthy

I just love to shop. If I could, I would shop every single day in every single store and spend all of my money which, you know, I do anyway.

Ariana Grande

Wind to a sailor is what money is to life on shore.

Sterling Hayden

Disasters happen. We still have no way to eliminate earthquakes, wildfires, hurricanes, floods or droughts. We cope as best we can by fortifying ourselves against danger with building codes and levees, and by setting aside money to clean up afterwards.

Seth Shostak

The only football players in my time were fellows who really loved to play football. They were not in it for the money. There wasn't much money there. They would have played football for nothing.

Red Grange

I always try to be smart. I try to treat all the money I'm making like it's the last time I'm going to make it.

Eminem

Bank failures are caused by depositors who don't deposit enough money to cover losses due to mismanagement.

Dan Quayle

Money and women. They're two of the strongest things in the world. The things you do for a woman you wouldn't do for anything else. Same with money.

Satchel Paige

I'm looking for backing for an unauthorized auto-biography that I am writing. Hopefully, this will sell in such huge numbers that I will be able to sue myself for an extraordinary amount of money and finance the film version in which I will play everybody.

David Bowie

You aren't wealthy until you have something money can't buy.

Garth Brooks

I don't know what your childhood was like, but we didn't have much money. We'd go to a movie on a Saturday night, then on Wednesday night my parents would walk us over to the library. It was such a big deal, to go in and get my own book.

Robert Redford

I, and others like me - trap stars - we always considered

ourselves Robin Hoods: we go out and get the money. Just think, if you was in the village and you a hunter, you take pride in going out to hunt the prey and bring it back for the village to eat. In our situation, we took pride in getting money so that the hood could eat.

Young Jeezy

Acting never was about the money for me... Maybe in 10 years, I'll be able to appreciate the fact that I am financially stable and independent and I don't have to make bad choices. I can be very picky.

Emma Watson

Studying is something I really love doing, and I just hope to have enough money for tuition.

Alexandra Kosteniuk

There aren't many downsides to being rich, other than paying taxes and having relatives asking for money. But being famous, that's a 24 hour job right there.

Bill Murray

Enthusiasm is the greatest asset you can possess, for it can take you further than money, power or influence.

Dada Vaswani

The problem that Robin Hood had with the Sheriff of Nottingham was the Sheriff of Nottingham used the power of taxation to steal all his money. It wasn't that the Sheriff was rich: the Sheriff was the government, and all the money he had was stolen. The government ought not to be in the business of making some people rich at the expense of others.

Grover Norquist

The U.N.'s impartiality allows it to negotiate and operate in some of the toughest places in the world. And time and again, studies have shown that U.N. peacekeeping is far more effective and done with far less money than what any government can do on its own.

Ban Ki-moon

The way we're really going to grow the economy is to invest in people, to invest in innovation, to have the federal government put money in the kind of research that will create the new high-technology, biotechnology industries that will create the millions of new jobs.

Joe Lieberman

I considered going into business or becoming a lawyer - not for the money, but for the thrill of problem-solving.

Lisa Randall

It's really unfair to working women in America who read celebrity news and think, 'Why can't I lose weight when I've had a baby?' Well, everyone you're reading about has money for a trainer and a chef. That doesn't make it realistic.

Rachel Zoe

If money, education, and honesty will not bring to me as much privilege, as much equality as they bring to any American citizen, then they are to me a curse, and not a blessing.

John Hope

America... just a nation of two hundred million used car salesmen with all the money we need to buy guns and no qualms about killing anybody else in the world who tries to make us uncomfortable.

Hunter S. Thompson

People say that money is not the key to happiness, but I

always figured if you have enough money, you can have a key made.

Joan Rivers

Run for your life from any man who tells you that money is evil. That sentence is the leper's bell of an approaching looter.

Ayn Rand

You use your money to buy privacy because during most of your life you aren't allowed to be normal.

Johnny Depp

Let advertisers spend the same amount of money improving their product that they do on advertising and they wouldn't have to advertise it.

Will Rogers

If our soldiers are not overburdened with money, it is not because they have a distaste for riches; if their lives are not unduly long, it is not because they are disinclined to longevity.

Sun Tzu

Money can't buy you happiness but it does bring you a more pleasant form of misery.

Spike Milligan

America believes in education: the average professor earns more money in a year than a professional athlete earns in a whole week.

Evan Esar

Money, like vodka, turns a person into an eccentric.

Anton Chekhov

Money may not buy happiness, but it can damn well give it!

Freddie Mercury

I have not been that wise. Health I have taken for granted. Love I have demanded, perhaps too much and too often. As for money, I have only realized its true worth when I didn't have it.

Hedy Lamarr

If we don't change from a world society that worships money and power to one that worships compassion and generosity, I think we'll be extinct by mid-century. I don't say that as an alarmist or as a pessimist.

Patch Adams

I think it would be cool if you were writing a ransom note on your computer, if the paper clip popped up and said, 'Looks like you're writing a ransom note. Need help? You should use more forceful language, you'll get more money.'

Demetri Martin

If a patron buys from an artist who needs money, the patron then makes himself equal to the artist; he is building art into the world; he creates.

Ezra Pound

The only point in making money is, you can tell some big shot where to go.

Humphrey Bogart

The great trouble with baseball today is that most of the

players are in the game for the money and that's it, not for the love of it, the excitement of it, the thrill of it.

Ty Cobb

My father used to always say to me that, you know, if a guy goes out to steal a loaf of bread to feed his family, they'll give him 10 years, but a guy can do white-collar crime and steal the money of thousands and he'll get probation and a slap on the wrist.

Jesse Ventura

Social enables word of mouth at an unprecedented scale. Its most powerful effect, through reviews and recommendations, is to put product quality and value for money as the key to success in commerce. Social brings a level of transparency that prevents marketers from advertising their way to success without underlying product quality.

Roelof Botha

The only reason to do business is to make money; that's the only reason for doing business.

Kevin O'Leary

I'm not that lazy, but I don't need that much money. I lead a fairly simple life.

Karl Pilkington

Some people start modeling because they want to be models and they want the parties and the recognition, and then there are people like me. I come from a simple family, and for me getting into modeling was a chance to make money and create a business.

Gisele Bundchen

You make your first album, you make some money, and you feel like you still have to show face, like 'I still go to the projects.' I'm like, why? Your job is to inspire people from your neighborhood to get out. You grew up there. What makes you think it's so cool?

Jay-Z

A lot of people feel trapped by circumstance, by the expectations of others or the perception that they need a lot of money. They would like to have a different direction in their lives, but they're held back by fear or desires that are incompatible with that freedom.

Roz Savage

And I think the more money you put in people's hands, the more they will spend. And if they don't spend it, they invest it. And investing it is another way of creating jobs. It puts money into mutual funds or other kinds of banks that can go out and make loans, and we need to do that.

Michael Bloomberg

To make an embarrassing admission, I like video games. That's what got me into software engineering when I was a kid. I wanted to make money so I could buy a better computer to play better video games - nothing like saving the world.

Elon Musk

If you don't have the money management skills yet, using a debit card will ensure you don't overspend and rack up debt on a credit card.

T. Harv Eker

Family and God - that is what's important. Money, cars, those are things that come and go.

Fabrice Muamba

To bring out a new technology for consumers first, you

just had a very long road to go down to try to find people who actually would pay money for something.

Marc Andreesen

Polio's pretty special because once you get an eradication, you no longer have to spend money on it; it's just there as a gift for the rest of time.

Bill Gates

Good nature is worth more than knowledge, more than money, more than honor, to the persons who possess it.

Henry Ward Beecher

My restaurants are never opened on Thanksgiving; I want my staff to spend time with their family if they can. My feeling is, if I can't figure out how to make money the rest of the year so that my workers can enjoy the holidays, then I don't deserve to be an owner.

Michael Symon

No one in this world, so far as I know - and I have searched the records for years, and employed agents to help me - has ever lost money by underestimating the intelligence of the great masses of the plain people.

H. L. Mencken

What is a normal childhood? We weren't rich, we were pretty middle-class. My dad survived from job to job; with him taking care of so many relatives, he couldn't save any money.

Charlie Sheen

I went to the bank and asked to borrow a cup of money. They said, 'What for?' I said, 'I'm going to buy some sugar.'

Steven Wright

To fulfill a dream, to be allowed to sweat over lonely labor, to be given a chance to create, is the meat and potatoes of life. The money is the gravy.

Bette Davis

One must beware of ministers who can do nothing without money, and those who want to do everything with money.

Indira Gandhi

It doesn't take money to turn off the television and cultivate real bonding time.

Marianne Williamson

We need your help. I need your help. We need money for research. It may not save my life. It may save my children's life. It may save someone you love. And it's very important.

Jim Valvano

Money is the root of all evil, and yet it is such a useful root that we cannot get on without it any more than we can without potatoes.

Louisa May Alcott

In January we start saving money, getting out of credit card debt, funding our retirement accounts, and we're doing wonderful. Then, every single year like clockwork, starting in November, all of you fall into this trap that says, 'I have to buy this gift... I can't show up at this party and not have something for everybody.'

Suze Orman

If you make time each month to give your money some attention, you'll start the next year in fabulous financial shape.

Suze Orman

I don't want to waste anyone's time or money. I want to give people some truth and positive heart lift.

Mos Def

I never minded flying cheap. I always said to myself, 'Taking this flight saves enough money to rescue four dogs, or six cats, or will let me make a difference to the one woman saving chimps in Cameroon.'

Elayne Boosler

The thing that surprised me the most is just how much money women that weren't rich were paying for their hair. When you're in a beauty parlor in Harlem next to abandoned buildings and somebody's paying five grand for a weave, that's a bit much.

Chris Rock

They still have some money, and they have needs to supply. They must begin immediately to pool their earnings and organize industries to participate in supplying social and economic demands.

Carter G. Woodson

Human beings are much bigger than just making money.

Muhammad Yunus

When you put money directly to a problem, it makes a good headline. It makes a good campaign slogan. You get to claim that you've engaged in these activities within an election cycle. But certain investments take longer than an election cycle.

Neil deGrasse Tyson

I was part of the first generation of girls and women to be educated and go to grammar school even if we didn't have much money. Then that generation went, 'OK, great', and went into medicine or the police, and hit this wall of discrimination from older men who hadn't caught up.

Helen Mirren

I don't do this for the money, I don't do it for record sales, I don't really care about that, I just want to make beats.

David Guetta

Money is a very important tool to make a big difference in

people's life. It is positive or negative depending on the values.

Shiv Khera

If owning stocks is a long-term project for you, following their changes constantly is a very, very bad idea. It's the worst possible thing you can do, because people are so sensitive to short-term losses. If you count your money every day, you'll be miserable.

Daniel Kahneman

Here in the big city people spend their time thinking about work and about money; they don't give some value to friendships and it can be depressing.

Adriana Lima

I hope I'm in a position to make stuff that I really want to make as opposed to stuff that I just have to make for money reasons, or to sustain a certain marquee value.

Paul Walker

What's hurting the U.S. economy is total government spending. The deficit is an indicator that the government is spending so much money that it can't even get around to stealing all of the money that it wants to spend. But the tip of the iceberg is not what hit the Titanic - it was the 90 percent of the iceberg under water.

Grover Norquist

Today, the concept of business is to make money. Making money is the name of the business.

Muhammad Yunus

In this financial year we will be spending at least $1.5 billion on foreign aid and we cannot be sure that this money will be properly spent, as corruption and mismanagement in many of the recipient countries are legend.

Pauline Hanson

The price of every thing rises and falls from time to time and place to place; and with every such change the purchasing power of money changes so far as that thing goes.

Alfred Marshall

I never prayed for no money, and I never prayed for no fame. I said, 'I'll take care of that myself. You just keep me healthy and I'll do all I can to try to turn people around, to try to steer 'em in the right direction.' That's the whole trip in life, ya know.

Wolfman Jack

The tragedy is that there is so much more incentive - money - to destroy the ecology than there is to preserve it.

Paul Watson

I'm a huge, huge fan of photography. I have a small photography collection. As soon as I started to make some money, I bought my very first photograph: an Henri Cartier-Bresson. Then I bought a Robert Frank.

Annie Leibovitz

Matters of the heart are important to me. All this materialism and all the money and wealth are things that you don't take to the grave. One day you have it. The next day you don't.

Shari Arison

Pesticides came about after the first world war. Some brainy petrochemical money maker said, 'Hey, that mustard gas worked great on people, maybe we could dilute it down and spray it on our crops to deal with pests.'

Woody Harrelson

My youngest son's pre-school class was recently asked what their dads do for work. The responses were things like, my dad sells money, and my dad figures stuff out. My son said, 'I've never seen my dad do work.' It's true. Skateboarding doesn't seem like real work, but I'm proud of what I do.

Tony Hawk

Instead of dumping all my money on an independent film that nobody would watch and most people would make fun of behind my back, I decided, 'I'm just going to buy a house.'

Daniel Tosh

Our idea is to serve everybody, including people with little money.

Ingvar Kamprad

The press don't like to say nice things because nice is boring. It's much better to label me the devil. What we do is not brain surgery. We are entertainers, plain and simple, and we're responsible to bring that money back, to make a profit.

Michael Bay

Money plays an important role in football, but it is not the dominating factor. When Chelsea play a Carling Cup game in a small city, and it could result in a draw - the excitement, the spirit, the atmosphere - that's the real beauty of football in England.

Roman Abramovich

I don't want to make money, I just want to be wonderful.

Marilyn Monroe

I'd say it's been my biggest problem all my life... it's money. It takes a lot of money to make these dreams come true.

Walt Disney

You know, my main reaction to this money thing is that it's humorous, all the attention to it, because it's hardly the most insightful or valuable thing that's happened to me.

Steve Jobs

Every sale has five basic obstacles: no need, no money, no hurry, no desire, no trust.

Zig Ziglar

Money without brains is always dangerous.

Napoleon Hill

If you make any money, the government shoves you in the creek once a year with it in your pockets, and all that don't get wet you can keep.

Will Rogers

Every family should have the right to spend their money, after tax, as they wish, and not as the government dictates. Let us extend choice, extend the will to choose and the chance to choose.

Margaret Thatcher

I always was a rich person because money's not related to happiness.

Paulo Coelho

There are necessary evils. Money is an important thing in terms of representing freedom in our world. And now I have a daughter to think about. It's really the first time I've thought about the future and what it could be.

Johnny Depp

I think one of the most pervasive evils in this world is greed and acquiring money for money's sake. Once you have six houses and a plane, it's just about a number. It's never been anything I understood.

Kevin Bacon

It is easy to be independent when you've got money. But to be independent when you haven't got a thing, that's the Lord's test.

Mahalia Jackson

That's the trouble with being me. At this point, nobody gives a damn what my problem is. I could literally have a tumor on the side of my head and they'd be like, 'Yeah, big deal. I'd eat a tumor every morning for the kinda money you're pulling down.'

Jim Carrey

Why are people unemployed? Because there is no work. Why is there no work? Because people are not buying products and services. Why are people not buying products and services? Because they have no money. Why do people have no money? Because they are unemployed.

Craig Bruce

Assets put money in your pocket, whether you work or not, and liabilities take money from your pocket.

Robert Kiyosaki

Ridiculous yachts and private planes and big limousines won't make people enjoy life more, and it sends out terrible messages to the people who work for them. It would be so much better if that money was spent in Africa - and it's about getting a balance.

Richard Branson

Capitalism is using its money; we socialists throw it away.

Fidel Castro

If you are worried about job security and do not have an

adequate emergency fund (ideally eight months' worth of living expenses stashed away in a federally insured bank or credit union), you need to focus more on saving money than paying down the balance on your credit cards.

Suze Orman

Your goal should be to pay off your credit card bills in full at the end of each month and set aside money toward your emergency savings.

Suze Orman

I'd like to be rich. I'd like a lot of money to put into my physicals and to buy food for all my friends.

Syd Barrett

A majority, perhaps as many as 75 percent, of abortion clinics are in areas with high minority populations. Abortion apologists will say this is because they want to serve the poor. You don't serve the poor, however, by taking their money to terminate their children.

Alveda King

My family has very strong women. My mother never laughed at my dream of Africa, even though everyone else did because we didn't have any money, because Africa was the 'dark continent', and because I was a girl.

Jane Goodall

You can't pay enough money to... cure that feeling of being broken and confused.

Winona Ryder

I'm not interested in making money. It's just that with my talent, I'm cursed with it.

Noel Gallagher

Money does not guarantee success.

Jose Mourinho

You can make a lot of money in this game. Just ask my ex-wives. Both of them are so rich that neither of their husbands work.

Lee Trevino

There are some things that you can fulfil with money, but at the end of the day these are not the things that make you happy. It is the small things that make life good.

Sebastian Vettel

The secret of my success is that I make other people money. And, never ever, ever, ever be ashamed about trying to earn as much as possible for yourself, if the person you're working with is also making money. That's life!

Simon Cowell

If you've gone into a marriage and you haven't been clear about how you're going to handle money, how you want to raise kids, who is going to work or stay home or what have you, then you've set yourself up for failure.

Phil McGraw

People expected 'Jennifer's Body' to make so much money. But I was doubtful. The movie is about a man-eating, cannibalistic lesbian cheerleader, and that pretty much eliminates middle America. It's obviously a girl-power movie, but it's also about how scary girls are. Girls can be a nightmare.

Megan Fox

The money that goes into Social Security is not the government's money. it's your money. You paid for it.

Mitch McConnell

Money has no grey areas. You either make it or you lose it.

Kevin O'Leary

Soon we saw that money going to women brought much more benefit to the family than money going to the men. So we changed our policy and gave a high priority to women. As a result, now 96% of our four million borrowers in Grameen Bank are women.

Muhammad Yunus

Yeah, we shot ourselves in the foot right out of the gate. The guy who ran it at first misled pretty much everybody about how much capital we had. He said we had enough to go three years without making money, and we had enough to go three weeks.

Al Franken

Don't build a glass house if you're worried about saving money on heating.

Philip Johnson

Some people find an interest in making money, and though they appear to be slaving, many actually enjoy every minute of their work.

Walter Annenberg

The greatest power is not money power, but political power.

Walter Annenberg

My dad said if you become a tennis professional just make sure you get into the top hundred, because you have to make a little bit of money. You make a living so you can pay your coaching and, you know, your travels.

Roger Federer

I look at my annual budgets for everything and anything, and I look to see where I can save the most money on those items. Saving 30% to 50% buying in bulk - replenishable items from toothpaste to soup, or whatever I use a lot of - is the best guaranteed return on investment you can get anywhere.

Mark Cuban

Give tax breaks to large corporations, so that money can trickle down to the general public, in the form of extra jobs.

Andrew Mellon

Dating now is a lot like going shopping when you don't have any money. Even if you find the right thing, you can't do anything about it.

Joshua Harris

The faux now of Twitter updates and things pinging at you - all the pulses from digitality that we try to keep up with because we sense that there's something going on that we need to tap into - are artifacts, or symptoms of living in this atemporal reality. And it's not any worse than living in the 'time is money' reality that we're leaving.

Douglas Rushkoff

For example, if I make money, I put it in real estate. I always did very well. Location, location, location.

Ivana Trump

In school, my favorite subject was math. That's where I
learned to count money.

French Montana

When you print money, the money does not flow evenly
into the economic system. It stays essentially in the
financial service industry and among people that have
access to these funds, mostly well-to-do people. It does not
go to the worker.

Marc Faber

A lot of young musicians get the money at the wrong time.
They get it for something they don't feel great about, and
it'll make you feel so bad it'll destroy you and kill you.

Iggy Pop

Once the brokerage house, rather than the bank, became
the locus for American savings, that money would find its
way into the stock market, because the broker was
someone with a much higher tolerance for risk than the
banker.

Ron Chernow

I can make more generals, but horses cost money.

Abraham Lincoln

Time is more value than money. You can get more money, but you cannot get more time.

Jim Rohn

Government always finds a need for whatever money it gets.

Ronald Reagan

The rich are always going to say that, you know, just give us more money and we'll go out and spend more and then it will all trickle down to the rest of you. But that has not worked the last 10 years, and I hope the American public is catching on.

Warren Buffett

Never put your money against Cassius Clay, for you will never have a lucky day.

Muhammad Ali

To have done anything just for money is to have been truly idle.

Henry David Thoreau

Politics has become so expensive that it takes a lot of money even to be defeated.

Will Rogers

Success must never be measured by how much money you have.

Zig Ziglar

Speculation is only a word covering the making of money out of the manipulation of prices, instead of supplying goods and services.

Henry Ford

I don't mind saying, you know, that I don't take a salary from the church, and God has blessed me with more money than I could imagine from my books.

Joel Osteen

Friendship and money: oil and water.

Mario Puzo

Money demands that you sell, not your weakness to men's stupidity, but your talent to their reason.

Ayn Rand

It will be a great day when our schools have all the money they need, and our air force has to have a bake-sale to buy a bomber.

Robert Fulghum

When I get a little money I buy books; and if any is left I buy food and clothes.

Desiderius Erasmus

Time is more valuable than money, because time is irreplaceable.

John C. Maxwell

Money, it turned out, was exactly like sex, you thought of nothing else if you didn't have it and thought of other things if you did.

James A. Baldwin

I first had the idea of writing a popular book about the universe in 1982. My intention was partly to earn money to pay my daughter's school fees.

Stephen Hawking

The day, water, sun, moon, night - I do not have to purchase these things with money.

Plautus

We can all be successful and make money, but when we die, that ends. But when you are significant is when you help other people be successful. That lasts many a lifetime.

Lou Holtz

Money is like manure. You have to spread it around or it smells.

J. Paul Getty

I haven't been as wild with my money as somebody like me might have been. I've been very safe, very conservative with investments. I don't blow money. I don't have a ton of houses. I know things can go away. I've already had that experience.

Jim Carrey

The focus on my appearance has really surprised me. I've always been a size 14 to 16, I don't care about clothes, I'd rather spend my money on cigarettes and booze.

Adele

I'm not really interested in making money.

Steven Spielberg

What white man can say I never stole his land or a penny of his money? Yet they say that I am a thief.

Sitting Bull

My children were taught at an early age how money works and that it comes from hard work. They've been on a commission - not an allowance - since they were little. They learned that if they worked around the house, they got paid. If they didn't work, they didn't get paid.

Dave Ramsey

Always remember, money isn't everything - but also remember to make a lot of it before talking such fool nonsense.

Earl Wilson

The only thing money gives you is the freedom of not worrying about money.

Johnny Carson

The music business is motivated by money. Music is motivated by energy and feelings.

Erykah Badu

If I had been on 'Bowling for Dollars,' I'd wind up owing them money.

Ricki Lake

Artists usually don't make all that much money, and they often keep their artistic hobby despite the money rather than due to it.

Linus Torvalds

I shouldn't be near Vegas and have money in my pocket.

Adam Sandler

If you wake up deciding what you want to give versus what you're going to get, you become a more successful person. In other words, if you want to make money, you have to help someone else make money.

Russell Simmons

I had more clothes than I had closets, more cars than garage space, but no money.

Sammy Davis, Jr.

I'm tired of love; I'm still more tired of rhyme; but money gives me pleasure all the time.

Hilaire Belloc

With a fascist the problem is never how best to present the truth to the public but how best to use the news to deceive the public into giving the fascist and his group more money or more power.

Henry A. Wallace

Money is not the motivating force. It's nice to have money, but I don't live high. What I enjoy is running the business.

Rupert Murdoch

If I was a billionaire, I'd be smart with my money.

Bruno Mars

The function of the press in society is to inform, but its role in society is to make money.

A. J. Liebling

Conserving energy and thus saving money, reducing consumption of unnecessary products and packaging and shifting to a clean-energy economy would likely hurt the bottom line of polluting industries, but would undoubtedly have positive effects for most of us.

David Suzuki

I live by 'Earnin' and burnin'.' Meaning, I like to make money and spend it before I even have it. That's the way I live my life.

Will Ferrell

Money can't buy happiness.

Howard Hughes

I can walk through the front door of any factory and out the back and tell you if it's making money or not. I can just tell by the way it's being run and by the spirit of the workers.

Harvey S. Firestone

I saw Deep Purple live once and I paid money for it and I thought, 'Geez, this is ridiculous.' You just see through all that sort of stuff. I never liked those Deep Purples or those sort of things. I always hated it. I always thought it was a poor man's Led Zeppelin.

Angus Young

I wasn't a hacker for the money, and it wasn't to cause damage.

Kevin Mitnick

There's only one thing money won't buy, and that is poverty.

Joe E. Lewis

My first job was in sixth grade, sweeping the clay tennis courts at the yacht club near my house, which I was not a member of. Always had to pay my own rent. But I don't really have any concept of how money works. I don't know how much things cost. Like a BMW. Or a quart of milk. It's embarrassing.

Chloe Sevigny

I think that commercials can really ruin a song. You know that the person sold the song for a good deal of money, and that was the tradeoff. But, music and picture can marry in a beautiful way, and the reverse also.

David Lynch

Kids are meant to believe that their stepping stone to massive money is 'The X Factor.' Luck is great, but most of life is hard work. We do not celebrate people who have made success out of serious hard work.

Iain Duncan Smith

Money is a scoreboard where you can rank how you're doing against other people.

Mark Cuban

I really wish there was some big brother conspiracy theory. I just think it's the ignorance of trying to make a dollar. That's what the networks have done and will continue to do. If anyone doesn't think that this is about making money, then they're crazy.

Montel Williams

Unless you are completely retired, earning money is the best form of wealth preservation.

Felix Dennis

Apple's goal isn't to make money. Our goal is to design and develop and bring to market good products.

Jonathan Ive

As a general thing, I have not 'duped the world' nor attempted to do so... I have generally given people the worth of their money twice told.

P. T. Barnum

Behavioral economists have shown that a sizable percentage of people are willing to pay real money to punish people who are taking from a common pot but not contributing to it. Just to insure that shirkers get what they deserve, we are prepared to make ourselves poorer.

James Surowiecki

In an ideal world, the amount of money we spend on medical research to prevent or cure a disease would be proportional to its seriousness and the number of people who suffer from it.

Peter Singer

I love food: biscuits and gravy, cheese grits, spaghetti and meatballs, chicken-fried steak with white gravy... but my favorite dish is my wife's beanie weenie cornbread casserole. It's so good. It sounds stupid, but if you eat it, it's heaven. Of course, it's only something you can eat if you've got a lot of money.

Larry the Cable Guy

I own about 300 pairs of shoes. When I start to go over 300, I have mini-sales from my closet and give the money to charity. It's my way of recycling; I feel like I can give back to the universe.

Stacy London

The money's the same, whether you earn it or scam it.

Bobby Heenan

I can't think of anything off the top of my head that seems more important than something designed to raise money to keep something going that keeps IV drug users from dying.

Elliott Smith

Most financiers, corporate lawyers, lobbyists, and management consultants are competing with other financiers, lawyers, lobbyists, and management consultants in zero-sum games that take money out of one set of pockets and put it into another.

Robert Reich

My philosophy has always been, 'do what you love and the money will follow.'

Amy Weber

I don't mind rude people. I want people that I can make money with, so if their executional abilities are good, and they're arrogant and rude, I don't care.

Kevin O'Leary

So much business is based on the belief that we should do whatever we can within legal limits to make as much money as we can. Ben & Jerry's was based on values, and we try to operate a business that not just sells ice cream but partners with all our stakeholders - whether that's suppliers or customers - to bring about a more sustainable world.

Jerry Greenfield

Bach and Beethoven, all of them, they had to write something to please the upper structure, those with money and power.

Sun Ra

In constant pursuit of money to finance campaigns, the political system is simply unable to function. Its deliberative powers are paralyzed.

John Rawls

Price is rarely the most important thing. A cheap product might sell some units. Somebody gets it home and they feel great when they pay the money, but then they get it home and use it and the joy is gone.

Tim Cook

It's easy to love yourself when you feel good enough, when you feel special enough, when you're loved enough, when you have enough money, and you're appreciated.

Debbie Ford

I think space, architectural space, is my thing. It's not about facade, elevation, making image, making money. My passion is creating space.

Peter Zumthor

Money has always been a particular problem for revolutionaries and anti-capitalists. What will money look like 'after the revolution'? How will it function? Will it exist at all? It's hard to answer the question if you don't know what money actually is. Proposing to eliminate it entirely seems utopian and naive.

David Graeber

I have mixed feelings about those sorts of things. When I see it done by interesting young people, I think it's very valid. But when established photographers, people in their forties, copy me and get a lot of money, well, I find that to be very stupid.

Helmut Newton

The changing nature of money is only one facet of the financial services revolution.

Scott Cook

When I first moved to L.A., I didn't have a lot of money to join a gym or take classes, so I improvised. My sister and I went to the library and looked over their DVD collection and discovered Neena and Veena, these Egyptian twins who have a whole series of belly dancing routines. We did them all.

AnnaLynne McCord

Fashion is more about taste than money - you have to understand your body and tailor clothes to your needs; it's all about the fit. I do the alterations myself - I'm quite a seamstress - it's the influence of my Hungarian mother.

Carmen Dell'Orefice

In an ideal world, nobody's work would be just about the money. People could pursue excellence in what they do, take pride in achievement, and derive meaning from knowing that their work improved the lives of others.

Barry Schwartz

I like to think that people who really know me understand I am the same person - and that is something I will always fight to maintain. Obviously the money is there, but I want to stay the same. At the same time, I want my son to enjoy what I didn't have. My father-in-law often looks at all the toys and games Benjamin has.

Sergio Aguero

Money isn't the most important thing in life, but it's reasonably close to oxygen on the 'gotta have it' scale.

Zig Ziglar

A man is usually more careful of his money than he is of his principles.

Ralph Waldo Emerson

Remember that credit is money.

Benjamin Franklin

Pretty much, Apple and Dell are the only ones in this industry making money. They make it by being Wal-Mart.

We make it by innovation.

Steve Jobs

I try to treat all the money I'm making like it's the last time
I'm going to make it.

Eminem

Don't bring your need to the marketplace, bring your skill.
If you don't feel well, tell your doctor, but not the
marketplace. If you need money, go to the bank, but not
the marketplace.

Jim Rohn

Prospering just doesn't have to do with money.

Joel Osteen

Don't matter how much money you got, there's only two
kinds of people: there's saved people and there's lost
people.

Bob Dylan

Of course, to have money is just great because you can do

what you think is important to you. I always was a rich person because money's not related to happiness.

Paulo Coelho

You may never get to that perfect world that you're waiting for where everything's going to be perfect and you got that much money and your house paid off.

Joel Osteen

When the federal government spends more each year than it collects in tax revenues, it has three choices: It can raise taxes, print money, or borrow money. While these actions may benefit politicians, all three options are bad for average Americans.

Ron Paul

Money and women are the most sought after and the least known about of any two things we have.

Will Rogers

One day a guy tried to rob me on the street, and I had no money. So I charged him.

Steven Wright

He who receives money in trust to administer for the benefit of its owner, and uses it either for his own interest or against the wishes of its rightful owner, is a thief.

Jose Marti

Because parents have power over children. They feel they have to do what their parents say. But the love of money is the root of all evil. And this is a sweet child. And to see him turn like this, this isn't him. This is not him.

Michael Jackson

There's so little money in my bank account, my scenic checks show a ghetto.

Phyllis Diller

Money doesn't talk, it swears.

Bob Dylan

Asking people for money is giving them the opportunity to put their resources at the disposal of the Kingdom.

Henri Nouwen

I am essentially a hack, a commercial person. If I had a hobby, I would immediately make money on it or abandon it.

Orson Welles

Our only real hope for democracy is that we get the money out of politics entirely and establish a system of publicly funded elections.

Noam Chomsky

My mom was a single mother, raising my sister and me. My mom has an incredible talent for living in the world without traditional structure, and her friend, who was in advertising, put me in a commercial when I was five. It was just to make money.

Gaby Hoffmann

It costs a lot of money to look this cheap.

Dolly Parton

People who identify themselves as conservatives donate money to charity more often than people who identify themselves as liberals. They donate more money and a higher percentage of their incomes.

Thomas Sowell

The sinews of war are infinite money.

Marcus Tullius Cicero

I have plenty of money, unlike other Hollywood celebrities or athletes that have not invested well.

Arnold Schwarzenegger

Money is kind of a base subject. Like water, food, air and housing, it affects everything yet for some reason the world of academics thinks it's a subject below their social standing.

Robert Kiyosaki

Getting money is not all a man's business: to cultivate kindness is a valuable part of the business of life.

Samuel Johnson

Economy does not lie in sparing money, but in spending it

wisely.

Thomas Huxley

I wanted to have money; I wanted to be special; I wanted people to like me; I wanted to be famous.

Ellen DeGeneres

To the eyes of a miser a guinea is more beautiful than the sun, and a bag worn with the use of money has more beautiful proportions than a vine filled with grapes.

William Blake

The shortest period of time lies between the minute you put some money away for a rainy day and the unexpected arrival of rain.

Jane Bryant Quinn

Money is power, and in that government which pays all the public officers of the states will all political power be substantially concentrated.

Andrew Jackson

I believe that sex is one of the most beautiful, natural, wholesome things that money can buy.

Steve Martin

I don't believe the most successful people are the ones who got the best grades, got into the best schools, or made the most money.

Ben Stein

The money can be a hindrance to someone like me because the danger is that you start thinking, 'Is that a $20 million take?' That kind of thing, and being self-critical.

Jim Carrey

I've had an exciting time; I married for love and got a little money along with it.

Rose Kennedy

How friendly all men would be one with another, if no regard were paid to honour and money! I believe it would be a remedy for everything.

Saint Teresa of Avila

I'm a cash flow guy. If it doesn't make me money today, forget about it.

Robert Kiyosaki

I'm always amazed at how many people assume a business has to lose money before it makes money.

Robert Kiyosaki

Admittedly, a homosexual can be conditioned to react sexually to a woman, or to an old boot for that matter. In fact, both homo - and heterosexual experimental subjects have been conditioned to react sexually to an old boot, and you can save a lot of money that way.

William S. Burroughs

Like anything else that happens on its own, the act of writing is beyond currency. Money is great stuff to have, but when it comes to the act of creation, the best thing is not to think of money too much. It constipates the whole process.

Stephen King

New York City is a great monument to the power of money and greed... a race for rent.

Frank Lloyd Wright

Money will buy a pretty good dog, but it won't buy the wag of his tail.

Josh Billings

No, not rich. I am a poor man with money, which is not the same thing.

Gabriel Garcia Marquez

I'll bet there are a lot of artists that nobody hears about who just make more money than anybody. The people that do all the sculptures and paintings for big building construction. We never hear about them, but they make more money than anybody.

Andy Warhol

God help me if I ever do another movie with an explosion in it. If you see me in a movie where stuff is exploding you'll know I've lost all my money.

Ben Affleck

This 90/10 rule holds true in almost anything financial.

Take the game of golf, for example. Ten percent of the professional golfers make 90 percent of the money.

Robert Kiyosaki

It costs governments money to keep fuel prices low. Oil-rich Yemen, for instance, devotes 9 percent of its GDP to making sure its people don't riot when oil prices rise.

Robert Kiyosaki

Find something in life that you love doing. If you make a lot of money, that's a bonus, and if you don't, you still won't hate going to work.

Jeff Foxworthy

Nothing that is God's is obtainable by money.

Tertullian

Who controls the issuance of money controls the government!

Nathan Meyer Rothschild

Our American friends offer us money, arms, and advice.

We take the money, we take the arms, and we decline the advice.

Moshe Dayan

The only way not to think about money is to have a great deal of it.

Edith Wharton

I'm not anti-middle-class in the slightest. Look at me! I am very pro people putting time and money and effort into trying to improve the world.

J. K. Rowling

To buy very good wine nowadays requires only money. To serve it to your guests is a sign of fatigue.

William F. Buckley, Jr.

Money is in some respects life's fire: it is a very excellent servant, but a terrible master.

P. T. Barnum

Advertising: the science of arresting the human

intelligence long enough to get money from it.

Stephen Leacock

Politics isn't about big money or power games; it's about the improvement of people's lives.

Paul Wellstone

But human nature dictates that there will always be cheaters. That's inevitable. Where there's money involved and glory, there are going to be people that cheat, and there will always be ways to cheat.

David Millar

There are three reasons for becoming a writer: the first is that you need the money; the second that you have something to say that you think the world should know; the third is that you can't think what to do with the long winter evenings.

Quentin Crisp

Is it not odd that the only generous person I ever knew, who had money to be generous with, should be a stockbroker.

Percy Bysshe Shelley

If we think we have ours and don't owe any time or money or effort to help those left behind, then we are a part of the problem rather than the solution to the fraying social fabric that threatens all Americans.

Marian Wright Edelman

We need transparency in government spending. We need to put each government expenditure online so every Floridian can see where their tax money is being spent.

Marco Rubio

If time is money, it seems moral to save time, above all one's own, and such parsimony is excused by consideration for others. One is straight-forward.

Theodor Adorno

I've never really had a hobby, unless you count art, which the IRS once told me I had to declare as a hobby since I hadn't made money with it.

Laurie Anderson

Goddam money. It always ends up making you blue as hell.

J. D. Salinger

All I knew growing up was that my father was married to and loved my momma, period. He worked hard, made some money, and put it on the dresser. She spent it on the family, and he went out and earned some more. He taught me the most about love.

Steve Harvey

If you hire people just because they can do a job, they'll work for your money. But if you hire people who believe what you believe, they'll work for you with blood, sweat, and tears.

Simon Sinek

The three biggest fashion mistakes are cheap suits, shoes, and shirts. Spend your money on something good.

Donatella Versace

I'm not trying to make friends, I'm trying to make money.

Kevin O'Leary

Markets are constantly in a state of uncertainty and flux and money is made by discounting the obvious and betting on the unexpected.

George Soros

I wanted to be a pharmacist. I liked the way our local pharmacist was always dressed in a nice white coat; he looked very calm, you'd give him money, and he'd give you something that you wanted to buy.

Walter Matthau

Starting out to make money is the greatest mistake in life. Do what you feel you have a flair for doing, and if you are good enough at it, the money will come.

Greer Garson

One thing I know about the rich, being rich, is that you can take money from me and tomorrow, I'm still going to be rich.

Lewis Black

I actually think that the economy has got some positives.

It's got the market. It's got consumer confidence and it's got banks throwing - I mean central bankers throwing money at it around the world.

Jack Welch

I support many organizations that I feel are doing the right thing, like Alonzo Mourning's foundation, Alicia Keys' foundation, the Make-a-Wish Foundation, and other well-established foundations. I kick out a lot of time and money wherever I can.

Queen Latifah

There are probably several hundred thousand if we narrow the definition to include only those who in their search for money and power are ruthless and deceitful.

Henry A. Wallace

Often people attempt to live their lives backwards; they try to have more things, or more money, in order to do more of what they want, so they will be happier.

Margaret Young

I don't use a debit card. The safest thing is a credit card because you're using the bank's money. If someone accesses your information, they are stealing the bank's money, not yours.

Frank Abagnale

If you really believe that you're making a difference and that you can leave a legacy of better schools and jobs and safer streets, why would you not spend the money? The objective is to improve the schools, bring down crime, build affordable housing, clean the streets - not to have a fair fight.

Michael Bloomberg

It would be great if firefighters across the country had the guarantee that they would be making enough money to support their family right from the get-go, but that's not the case.

Denis Leary

Until we totally change the way we elect our leaders, until we remove private money from public campaigns, lying will be the de facto method of governance in this country.

Peter Schuyler

To be poor does not mean you lack the means to extend

charity to another. You may lack money or food, but you have the gift of friendship to overwhelm the loneliness that grips the lives of so many.

Stanley Hauerwas

Offer someone the opportunity to rebuild a company or reinvent an industry as the primary incentive, and it will attract those drawn to the challenge first and the money second.

Simon Sinek

I don't know if it's the sunshine, or the fact that I actually have a job, but I do like L.A. a lot. In New York, it can be gray and rainy and cold, and you still don't have any money, and you feel like a bad Dickens character.

Rich Sommer

The curse of covetousness is that it destroys manhood by substituting money for character.

Lucy Larcom

Hollywood is so fake and people need to realize that people are just people, and you, too, don't need to be born into something or have money or have whatever product someone is hawking on you.

Katy Perry

And it turns out that tribes, not money, not factories, that can change our world, that can change politics, that can align large numbers of people. Not because you force them to do something against their will. But because they wanted to connect.

Seth Godin

Abraham Lincoln comes from nothing, has no education, no money, lives in the middle of nowhere on the frontier. And despite the fact that he suffers one tragedy and one setback after another, through sheer force of will, he becomes something extraordinary: not only the president but the person who almost single-handedly united the country.

Seth Grahame-Smith

The real key to making money in stocks is not to get scared out of them.

Peter Lynch

The black groups that boycott certain films would do better

to get the money together to make the films they want to see, or stay in church and leave us to our work.

Richard Pryor

Many women have asked me if it is possible to have a well-built wardrobe on a limited budget. 'Money,' I tell them, 'is no guarantee of taste, and an overstuffed wardrobe is often as bare as a skeleton when it comes to wearable apparel.'

Edith Head

I turned down twelve films last year... Huge money films, but I had no respect for the writer or the work.

Shia LaBeouf

I still think of that guy I was without a wife or kids, and I still want to entertain that guy. The lonely guy, the frustrated guy, the guy with no money - this is the guy who needs to laugh.

Larry David

I don't pay good wages because I have a lot of money; I have a lot of money because I pay good wages.

Robert Bosch

Prestige is the shadow of money and power.

C. Wright Mills

The only thing I like about rich people is their money.

Nancy Astor

When museums are built these days, architects, directors, and trustees seem most concerned about social space: places to have parties, eat dinner, wine-and-dine donors. Sure, these are important these days - museums have to bring in money - but they gobble up space and push the art itself far away from the entrance.

Jerry Saltz

No illusion is more crucial than the illusion that great success and huge money buy you immunity from the common ills of mankind, such as cars that won't start.

Larry McMurtry

When I was growing up, I thought I'd be a lot happier if I was famous and successful and if I had money.

Russell Brand

My indifference to money and my spendthrift ways are disgraceful. You have no idea how reckless I am; how often I practically throw money out of the window. I am always making good resolutions, but the next minute I forget and give the waiter eightpence.

Robert Schumann

A savvy entrepreneur will not always look for investment money, first.

Daymond John

Safe care saves lives and saves money. Adverse events like high levels of infection, blood clots or falls in hospital, emergency readmissions and pressure sores cost the NHS billions of pounds every year. There is a serious human cost, too, with patients ending up injured, or even dead. Most are avoidable with the right care.

Andrew Lansley

It's wrong for a guy to have no personality, no heart. Because I don't care about style or money.

Adriana Lima

When people evaluate their life, they compare themselves to a standard of what a successful life is, and it turns out that standard tends to be universal: People in Togo and Denmark have the same idea of what a good life is, and a lot of that has to do with money and material prosperity.

Daniel Kahneman

I made a tremendous amount of money on real estate. I'll take real estate rather than go to Wall Street and get 2.8 percent. Forget about it.

Ivana Trump

Disasters redistribute money from taxpayers to construction workers, from insurance companies to homeowners, and even from those who once lived in the destroyed city to those who replace them. It's remarkable that this redistribution can happen so smoothly and quickly, with devastated regions reinventing themselves in a matter of months.

James Surowiecki

I never deviated from my grim determination to someday have all the money I needed and wanted.

Taylor Caldwell

Crafts make us feel rooted, give us a sense of belonging and connect us with our history. Our ancestors used to create these crafts out of necessity, and now we do them for fun, to make money and to express ourselves.

Phyllis George

The book 'Do You!' is about your inner voice. And when you connect to that voice then you - then the freedom comes. And we're only here to be happy. So happy makes money. Money doesn't make happy.

Russell Simmons

I realise that I do not change the course of history. I am an actor, I do a movie, that's the end of it. You have to realise we are just clowns for hire. After I had success it was great, at first, not to worry about money. It was on my mind when I was growing up.

Leonardo DiCaprio

The rich man who gives, steals twice over. First he steals the money and then the hearts of men.

Edvard Munch

I think I'm actually quite a materialistic person, I value what it takes to make a car or build a nice house. Money does change things, but how it changes people depends on how they react to it.

Roland Gift

I didn't want to be short. I've tried to pretend that being a short guy didn't matter. I tried to make up for being short by affecting a strut, by adopting the voice of a much bigger man, by spending more money than I made, by tipping double or triple at bars and restaurants, by dating tall, beautiful women.

Mickey Rooney

Don't just do something because it's a trendy idea and will make you a lot of money. The reason I say that is because any kind of venture involves going through difficult times. If you're doing something you are passionate about and really believe in, then that will carry you through.

Jerry Greenfield

Every single instance of a friend's insincerity increases our dependence on the efficacy of money.

William Shenstone

It almost goes without saying that when you are a startup, one of the first things you do is you start setting aside money to defend yourself from patent lawsuits, because any successful company, even moderately successful, is going to get hit by a patent lawsuit from someone who's just trying to look for a payout.

Charles Duhigg

I don't believe in men waiting until they are ready to die before using any of their money for helpful purposes.

George Eastman

If you have money and you have fame, but you don't have any confidence in your blackness, then it's all for nothing.

Paul Mooney

Small businesses provide 75 percent of new U.S. jobs and are the backbone of our economy, and no outdated ban should be keeping small business owners from collecting the same interest their money could earn if it were held by an individual.

Sue Kelly

You don't suffer, kill yourself and take the risks I take just for money. I love bike racing.

Greg LeMond

My mom did not have money. She was a single mom, on and off in periods between marriages. My husband, however, grew up on a wonderful farm in Tuscany, in Florence, and his family was so entertaining in terms of growing their own food and using the fruit of their land. We have very, very different experiences.

Debi Mazar

No money in this world could convince me to play for Liverpool. That's not a lack of respect for Liverpool supporters or the football club. It's respect for the Everton supporters. You just can't do that. It goes against everything that I stand for. No chance.

Timothy F. Cahill

Profits should be for a purpose. Profits should be productive. You should make money for producing benefits that make the world a better place. Making money is a good thing when it is made in service to humanity or the democracy.

Andrew Young

Don't worry about writing a book or getting famous or making money. Just lead an interesting life.

Michael Morpurgo

I need them, need them to give me a kick up the arse. Otherwise I'd just be sat-in getting fat, counting me money. It's good people living on your doorstep and looking through your bins. Gives you energy.

Liam Gallagher

My body is my art, and it's also the tool that I use to make money.

Sasha Grey

I mean I get loads of money, all from different sources. You give it to your accountant. They manage it. But you pay corporation tax. If you're then taking it out and spending it on yourself, you have to pay more.

Ken Livingstone

I make the most money, I think, in Russia and Paris, for the people of those countries are so willing to be amused, so eager to see something new and out of the ordinary.

Harry Houdini

My mother was a very wonderful woman. When she and my dad divorced, she moved to California and worked two jobs in the cannery at night and as a waitress during the day. But she saved enough money to establish a restaurant.

Dolores Huerta

I was born on a plantation, and things weren't so good. We didn't have any money. I never thought of the word 'poor' 'til I got to be a man, but when you live in a house that you can always peek out of and see what kind of day it is, you're not doing so well. And your rest room is not inside the house.

B. B. King

By pouring money and goods into devastated regions, foreign aid workers sometimes compound the disruption and debauch the survivors.

James Buchan

No race of barbarians ever existed yet offered up children for money.

Samuel Gompers

A journey by Sea and Land, Five Hundred Miles, is not undertaken without money.

Lewis Hallam

Now almost every artist outside of New York is connected with some school or some museum school, and even in New York the majority are. That's an interesting fact when you take the idea of making money, making a living selling paintings. Only a dozen or two painters do that.

Ad Reinhardt

No one goes into standup to make money. The frustration and rejection are just too much.

Jim Gaffigan

I am very picky with my career. I don't need to do it for the money or the fame. I'm very choosy, which is why I haven't played the typical role that people expect to see from someone of my stature and size, as the mean jock or the preppy. It's very easy to see me like that. That's why I go against it in different roles.

Kellan Lutz

I'm not ridiculously wealthy, but I don't squander money either.

Slash

A company has a greater responsibility than making money for its stockholders. We have a responsibility to our employees to recognize their dignity as human beings.

David Packard

There's no amount of money that makes you feel better when people think of you as a joke or a hack or a failure or ugly or stupid or morally empty.

Patrick Stump

You may not like the idea of putting money into a home when you're moving out. But it's demanded by the market. You need to show it off. You don't have to rip out the kitchen and bathroom. But maybe replace the tiles or the countertops. Get professional advice.

Barbara Corcoran

Don't forget, I'm 39. I didn't come here just for the money to impress myself. I'm not saying I am going to be dominating. I'm not saying I'm going to be good. But I can promise you I will do all the right things to play.

Jaromir Jagr

I had dropped out of school and was a runaway, so I didn't have family to fall back on if I didn't work. I didn't have a lot of other options of making money other than modeling.

Carre Otis

When Peru had a cholera outbreak in 1991, losses from tourism and agricultural revenue were three times greater than the total money spent on sanitation in the previous decade.

Rose George

I always feel like 'as long as I'm doin' what I love to do, the money's naturally gonna come.' When you start thinkin' business and you start thinkin' 'What's hot? What's the wave? Who is hot? Let's get at that person,' it becomes a point where you're tryin' to strategize to make money. And that's always a gamble.

Akon

You always hear the phrase, money doesn't buy you happiness. But I always in the back of my mind figured a lot of money will buy you a little bit of happiness. But it's not really true. I got a new car because the old one's lease expired.

Sergey Brin

I am a professional photographer because it is the best way I know to earn the money I require to take care of my wife and children.

Irving Penn

Because my dad's Chinese-American, and they're very concrete, he said, 'There's no money to be made in literature.' So he told me to go into the sciences. And I was a good girl. And I did what Daddy said. And that's how I ended up being a doctor. But you know, you just can't stamp out that desire to tell stories.

Tess Gerritsen

The difference now is that the paparazzi get paid fortunes. That's what motivates people; it's about the money, sadly, at anyone's expense.

David Cassidy

To me, money is independence. It gives you freedom to do

what you really want to do. It allows you to not be dependent on anyone or anything, and so you can be yourself and follow your passion.

Joe Mansueto

On 'Friday,' I had a big trailer, and we would have a barbecue going and music playing. It was a fun set. There was too much involved for 'The Hangover' to be a fun set. They're trying to get money.

Mike Epps

It is not about the money. It's the public service aspect. Absolutely, I think it has qualities of redemption. The city gets a second chance. I get a second chance.

John Rowland

Money is the great tool through whose means labor and skill become universally co-operative.

Leland Stanford

The great thing about American women is their energy and the way they love to dress. French women don't really dress; they are too conservative, as it's always a question of money. In America, women are powerful and strong, determined. If they want to be an object, they choose to be in control.

Jean Paul Gaultier

One could make money and get a career going with a low-budget horror film about killers attacking on holidays. It is always flattering to have somebody copy you.

John Carpenter

If there is a public perception at all, they see the producer as a big old guy who smokes a cigar and has lots of money and lots of power. That's not what a producer is and, if it ever was what a producer was, it certainly hasn't been for a long time.

Marshall Herskovitz

A common measure of poverty is how much money you have in relation to other people - that is useful as far as it goes, but that excludes the case of, say, a hunter in the rainforest who has no money but is not poor. And there can be a number of people with money but who can consider themselves unwanted or invisible or estranged from society.

William T. Vollmann

I could have made a small film and kept all the money from 'Life is Beautiful'. Instead, I spent more money than I had on 'Pinocchio', a very risky film.

Roberto Benigni

The law courts must appear as a threatening gesture toward secret vice. The bank must declare: here your money is secure and well looked after by honest people.

Adolf Loos

I'm making a case against how money managers are handling customers' money. The objective of the customer is not being met if the fund managers are diversifying their assets into hundreds of businesses. If they do this, they are typically performing close to the indexes. But that's not the way wealth is created.

Michael Lee-Chin

To be candid with you, free agency hurts all sports. It's great for athletes making an enormous amount of money. But to say it helps the sports, I don't believe that.

Jerry West

At a time when special interest money is being showered

on legislators in Washington, grassroots donors offer members of Congress a refreshing independence. The $25 and $50 donor is not looking for special favors. He or she is simply expecting their Congressman to go do the right thing.

John Sarbanes

I'm always impressed by how compassionate the gaming community can be when they have a cause and appreciate that they leverage our platform to raise money for those in need. We continue to encourage giving in support of important causes, including Extra Life 2012.

Emmett Shear

All my money is in a savings account. My dad has explained the stock market to me maybe 75 times. I still don't understand it.

John Mulaney

Sports betting is all about money management, so the most money won on one event is not the most important thing.

Bruce Dern

Money doesn't buy happiness. But happiness isn't

everything.

Jean Seberg

Imagine choosing a job not on money or even on career advancement, but as part of a life worth living.

Dale Dauten

After Scour, I started a company called Red Swoosh. The idea was to take those litigants who sued us for a huge amount of money and turn them into customers with the same technology. I wanted to get them to pay me. It was a revenge business.

Travis Kalanick

The early part of my career was the 1990s, and I was living in New York working as an actor. It was the world I was in. A lot of companies had a great deal of money.

Gaby Hoffmann

I agree with Balzac and 19th-century writers, black and white, who say, 'I write for money.' Yes, I think everybody should be paid handsomely; I insist on it, and I pay people who work for me, or with me, handsomely.

Maya Angelou

If you would know the value of money, go and try to borrow some.

Benjamin Franklin

The use of money is all the advantage there is in having it.

Benjamin Franklin

An actress is not a machine, but they treat you like a machine. A money machine.

Marilyn Monroe

Money won't make you happy... but everybody wants to find out for themselves.

Zig Ziglar

I actually thought that it would be a little confusing during the same period of your life to be in one meeting when you're trying to make money, and then go to another meeting where you're giving it away. I mean is it gonna erode your ability, you know, to make money? Are you gonna somehow get confused about what you're trying to do?

Bill Gates

We are the only real aristocracy in the world: the aristocracy of money.

George Bernard Shaw

Well-spent aid money is saving lives for a few thousand dollars per life saved.

Bill Gates

Money is usually attracted, not pursued.

Jim Rohn

Money has no utility to me beyond a certain point.

Bill Gates

Modern poets talk against business, poor things, but all of us write for money. Beginners are subjected to trial by market.

Robert Frost

My mom was on the United Way group that decides how to allocate the money and looks at all the different charities and makes the very hard decisions about where that pool of funds is going to go.

Bill Gates

Most people consider me an optimist because I laughingly state that I would take my last two dollars and buy a money belt.

Zig Ziglar

Money is like an arm or leg - use it or lose it.

Henry Ford

I don't believe we are supposed to go through life defeated and not having enough money to pay our bills or send our kids to college.

Joel Osteen

Talk is by far the most accessible of pleasures. It costs nothing in money, it is all profit, it completes our education, founds and fosters our friendships, and can be enjoyed at any age and in almost any state of health.

Robert Louis Stevenson

Successful people make money. It's not that people who make money become successful, but that successful people attract money. They bring success to what they do.

Wayne Dyer

I purposely don't talk about money, because people are already skeptical about TV preachers. But I do say that I want you to be blessed. To me, prosperity is having health, having great children, having peace, good relationships. It's not about the money.

Joel Osteen

I believe that God's dream is that we be successful in our careers, and that we be able to send our kids to college. I don't mean that everyone is going to be rich, and I preach a lot on blooming where you're planted. But I don't have the mindset that money is a bad thing.

Joel Osteen

I believe God, Jesus, died that we not just go to Heaven but that we excel in this life. I never think you make money your goal... God wants you to excel. Just keep Him in first place, and God will open up doors you never dreamed of.

Joel Osteen

If a person gets his attitude toward money straight, it will help straighten out almost every other area in his life.

Billy Graham

I don't mind saying, you know, that I don't take a salary from the church, and God has blessed me with more money than I could imagine from my books. It's been printed all over, so I don't feel like I am hiding anything.

Joel Osteen

If advertisers spent the same amount of money on improving their products as they do on advertising then they wouldn't have to advertise them.

Will Rogers

I'd have stopped writing years ago if it were for the money.

Paulo Coelho

Of course, to have money is just great because you can do what you think is important to you.

Paulo Coelho

I don't blame the players today for the money. I blame the owners. They started it. They wanna give it to 'em? More power to 'em.

Yogi Berra

It's morally wrong to allow a sucker to keep his money.

W. C. Fields

This is a wonderful planet, and it is being completely destroyed by people who have too much money and power and no empathy.

Alice Walker

Sometimes you have to make a movie to make money.

Robin Williams

Good jokes are gems. A good idea is hard to come by. I couldn't give them to someone else, even for money. It just wouldn't seem right.

Steven Wright

I think writing really helps you heal yourself. I think if you write long enough, you will be a healthy person. That is, if you write what you need to write, as opposed to what will make money, or what will make fame.

Alice Walker

Divorce is expensive. I used to joke they were going to call it 'all the money,' but they changed it to 'alimony.' It's ripping your heart out through your wallet.

Robin Williams

The chief value of money lies in the fact that one lives in a world in which it is overestimated.

H. L. Mencken

This film cost $31 million. With that kind of money I could have invaded some country.

Clint Eastwood

I believe enlightenment or revelation comes in daily life. I look for joy, the peace of action. You need action. I'd have stopped writing years ago if it were for the money.

Paulo Coelho

The trouble with our people is as soon as they got out of slavery they didn't want to give the white man nothing else. But the fact is, you got to give em something. Either your money, your land, your woman or your ass.

Alice Walker

You can't get rid of poverty by giving people money.

P. J. O'Rourke

Being willing to donate the taxpayers' money is not the same as being willing to put your own money where your mouth is.

Thomas Sowell

To be clever enough to get all that money, one must be stupid enough to want it.

Gilbert K. Chesterton

A woman must have money and a room of her own if she is to write fiction.

Virginia Woolf

I was so in love with the idea of making people laugh for a living that I didn't care what I had to do to get there. Or how much money I was going to make when I did get there.

Ron White

I do not suppose I shall be remembered for anything. But I don't think about my work in those terms. It is just as vulgar to work for the sake of posterity as to work for the sake of money.

Orson Welles

Because people have no thoughts to deal in, they deal cards, and try and win one another's money. Idiots!

Arthur Schopenhauer

Criminals are never very amusing. It's because they're failures. Those who make real money aren't counted as criminals. This is a class distinction, not an ethical problem.

Orson Welles

Our greatest lack is not money for any undertaking, but rather ideas, If the ideas are good, cash will somehow flow to where it is needed.

Robert H. Schuller

You never suffer from a money problem, you always suffer from an idea problem.

Robert H. Schuller